ENGLISH MYSTICS OF THE
FOURTEENTH CENTURY

English Mystics of the
Fourteenth   Century

By

T. W. COLEMAN

GREENWOOD PRESS, PUBLISHERS
WESTPORT, CONNECTICUT

Originally published in 1938
by The Epworth Press (Edgar C. Barton), London

First Greenwood Reprinting 1971

Library of Congress Catalogue Card Number 74-109723

SBN 8371-4213-X

Printed in the United States of America

CONTENTS

PREFACE

So many books on Mysticism are coming from the Press in these days, that perhaps a word is necessary to justify the appearance of another. I hope this work will find a welcome for the following reasons:

It is intended for the general reader; especially for those many thoughtful members of our Churches who would like to know something about these early English saints, but have been hesitant to consult the available books, because they feared they might be taken out of their depth. I have kept the needs of those readers in mind throughout. Hence, I have endeavoured to avoid the unnecessary use of unfamiliar and technical terms; and I have reduced discussions of theological points and psychological theories to the smallest compass. Had I tried to cut these out entirely, I should have been guilty of over-simplification, and that would have prevented a full and true presentation of the facts. What I have striven to do is to elucidate the lives and characters, the experiences and teachings of these saints, and to illustrate the various points brought out by quotations from their works. At times I have given extended extracts, because I thought that some of these beautiful passages might be valuable for devotional reading; they would certainly be most helpful for meditation at the time of prayer.

Then, I believe I am the first Free Churchman to issue a book on this subject. Members of other communions— Anglican, Roman, Quaker—have written ably about these Mystics; but I thought a Free Church interpretation might be of interest, even outside our own borders. I am

7

fairly sure that Free Churchmen will be surprised to find how much we have in common—in spirit, faith, and practice—with these pre-Reformation saints.

Again, this is the first time, so far as I know, that a whole volume has been entirely devoted to the fourteenth-century Mystics. This, in my opinion, is recognition they richly deserve. Moreover, they form such a distinct group in our national history, being so intimately related in their intellectual, spiritual, and devotional life, and in their forms of literary expression, that they seem to invite separate treatment of this kind.

It will be found that these English Mystics strike many great notes, but one of their greatest is Joy. If by God's goodness this book does anything to help in restoring that note to the religious life of to-day I shall be happy.

I should like to make, with real gratitude, the following acknowledgments for permission to give extracts—often very copious—from the various works named:

To Messrs. Chatto & Windus, publishers of *The Ancren Riwle*, and *The Cell of Self-Knowledge*.

To Mr. G. C. Heseltine, the editor and transcriber, and Messrs. Longmans, Green & Co., Ltd., the publishers, of *Selected Works of Richard Rolle*.

To Messrs. Methuen & Co., Ltd., publishers of *The Fire of Love*; to the Executors, and to Messrs. Methuen & Co., the publishers, of *Revelations of Divine Love*.

To Messrs. Burns, Oates & Washbourne, Ltd., publishers of *The Cloud of Unknowing*.

To The Art & Book Co., Ltd., publishers of *The Scale of Perfection*.

To Lieutenant-Colonel W. Butler-Bowdon, the owner of the manuscript, and Messrs. Jonathan Cape, Ltd., the publishers, of *The Book of Margery Kempe*.

To the many other authors and publishers from whose

works I have quoted, the titles of which appear in the footnotes.

Parts of Chapters I, III, VI, and VIII have appeared in issues of *The London Quarterly and Holborn Review*; I would express my thanks to the editor, the Rev. Leslie F. Church, B.A., Ph.D., for his consent for them to be included here.

T. W. COLEMAN.

April, 1938.

CHAPTER I

CHRISTIAN MYSTICISM

ALTHOUGH this book deals with English Mystics it may be helpful at the outset to say something about mysticism in general, especially as some readers may be approaching this subject for the first time.

In his still widely-read work, *Christian Mysticism*, first published thirty-eight years ago, Dr. Inge says, 'No word in our language—not even "Socialism"—has been employed more loosely than "Mysticism".'[1] In proof of that the erudite author collected in an Appendix from representative sources twenty-six definitions of this elusive term, the reading of which suggests the dreadful possibility that in this subject, with its jangle of tongues, we have a modern miniature of the Tower of Babel. A few years after, in her small but delightful volume, *A Little Book of Heavenly Wisdom*, Miss Gregory, with disarming *naïveté*, roundly asserts, 'Mysticism, in spite of innumerable definitions, has never been defined'.[2] Still further emphasizing this difficulty of definition, Dom Cuthbert Butler, in a masterly book, more recently published, entitled *Western Mysticism*, goes into greater detail: 'There is probably no more misused word in these days than "mysticism". It has come to be applied to many things of many kinds: to theosophy and Christian science; to spiritualism and clairvoyance; to demonology and witchcraft; to occultism and magic; to weird psychical experiences, if only they have some religious colour; to revelations and visions; to other-worldliness, or even mere

[1] p. 3.   [2] p. xviii.

dreaminess and impracticability in the affairs of life; to poetry and painting and music of which the motif is unobvious and vague. It has been identified with the attitude of the religious mind that cares not for dogma or doctrine, for Church or sacraments; it has been identified also with a certain outlook on the world—a seeing God in Nature, and recognizing that the material creation in various ways, symbolizes spiritual realities: a beautiful and true conception . . . but which is not mysticism according to its historical meaning. And, on the other side, the meaning of the term has been watered down: it has been said that the love of God is mysticism; or that mysticism is only the Christian life lived on a high level; or that it is Roman Catholic piety in extreme form.'[1]

These statements by authorities on the spiritual life might easily dismay a novice; he might be excused if he thought that the word we are studying should really be written 'misty-cism'. But while these quotations will show that the term has different connotations for different minds, they will also warn the beginner against coming to hasty and shallow judgements upon its meaning: a warning much needed by others besides beginners.

It will be an undoubted advantage however, if, at the commencement of our study, we can have in mind some reasonably clear idea of what is usually understood by this term: something to serve as a leading string to guide us through the labyrinth of definition and discussion. May I, therefore, without aiming at too great exactness, have the temerity to say that probably for most of us who to-day are interested in this subject, mysticism expresses the basic fact that man is made for fellowship with God. It is possible, as a glance at the twenty-six formulae given by Dr. Inge will indicate, to elaborate this definition to inordinate length and excessive subtlety; but in the end it would be found that these more verbose statements

[1] p. 2.

could be boiled down to this short and simple assertion, that God made man for Himself, and in the experience of that relationship is man's divinely-appointed destiny and the secret of his highest life. Thus the mystic is one who, availing himself of every point of contact, cultivates communion with God; and, by utilizing every proffer of Divine Love, ardently pursues his path along the way of prayer, till in the end he achieves union with God.[1]

From this it will be seen that we are all potential mystics. The difference between the ordinary believer and the mystic is not one of nature, it is a difference in the experience of Divine Love. Some make no effort to explore this Realm—the soul's Origin and Home. They do not grow in the grace and knowledge of our Lord and Saviour Jesus Christ; nor do they strive, through Him, for that purity of heart which enables them to see God. Hence they make no progress. Whereas the mystic brings all his interests and bends all his powers to this supreme and joyous task of seeking, beholding, and adoring Divine Love. This is put very attractively by another authority on the devout life: 'Contemplation is the queen and sovereign act among all the acts of the soul of man. For the perfect flower of the heart is the act of charity; and contemplation is charity or love when it is actual, constant, pure, and flowing under the pressure of the Holy

---

[1] As helping to give greater substance to 'the leading string', the following definitions may be of service; they are taken from well-known writers, each of whom, in his exposition of this subject, approaches it from one of three main points of view:

Dr. Inge comes by the philosophical path; he defines mysticism as, 'the attempt to realize, in thought and feeling, the immanence of the temporal in the eternal, and of the eternal in the temporal'. *Christian Mysticism*, p. 5.

Miss Underhill favours the psychological approach; she says, 'Mysticism is the art of union with Reality. The Mystic is a person who has attained that union in greater or less degree; or who aims at and believes in such attainment'. *Practical Mysticism*, p. 3.

Dom Cuthbert Butler prefers the highway of history: 'The term "mystical experience" could be usefully restricted to that experimental perception of God, however expressed, that is the real claim of the mystics in their higher states of contemplation and union.' *Western Mysticism*, p. lxxxiv.

Spirit. Contemplation is not ordinary prayer. Yet it is not one of those extraordinary gifts which ordinary souls may not aspire to. It is the very aim of the teaching of Father Baker and his school that "extraordinary" prayer should be an ordinary state for Christian souls; for priests, for religious, for devout lay folk, and for the poor and unlearned who love God with all their heart.'[1]

Let it not be assumed that this teaching reduces mysticism to mere spirituality; or that it elevates every earnest believer into a mystic. It is certainly impossible to say where the line has to be drawn between a sincere Christian and one who has reached that state of grace described as mystical, yet we are all conscious of the difference. I might be able to compose a little jingle, but no one would ever mistake me for a poet. You might paint a pretty picture, but even your most flattering friend would not suggest that your name deserved to be embellished with R.A. A man might study the stars, but merely because of that laudable interest he would not be called an astronomer. Many of us may try to lead a good life, and we may be keen in our endeavour to imitate Christ; but only those who push on to the goal of perfection, and attain in some degree likeness to the Beloved, can hope to rank amongst the Church's select saints—the mystics.[2] Actually, this selection is determined by consensus of opinion, and this opinion matures under the guidance of a few: those, who, because of their own attainments, are best able to judge. Before any one is granted this high title of sanctity he has to pass through searching tests.

We must keep in mind that our definition—broad as it is—relates particularly to Christian Mysticism. There is a cruder kind, lacking the austerity, the purity, and the

---

[1] From Bishop Hedley's *Prayer and Contemplation*, quoted in *Western Mysticism*, p. xxx. See, in addition, an interesting discussion in Bede Frost's *St. John of the Cross*, pp. 144–152.

[2] Dr. Inge puts this point very suggestively in the concluding essay of *Science, Religion, and Reality*, p. 385.

aesthetical qualities of the essential Christian type. It covers a vast range of thought and experience, and has strange and remote affiliations. Sometimes, even in those unpromising connexions, it is associated with the best products of our higher nature: goodness, knowledge, wisdom; courage, moral discipline, and spirituality of mind; but more often it provides opportunity for the exercise of man's baser powers. It may be linked with the hidden and unknown—the mysterious. It may be allied with demonology, necromancy, and spiritualism; with witchcraft, the occult, and black and white magic. At times it has been cradled in esoteric circles, and carried forward age after age by carefully selected agents; and from those circles have come reports of queer psychic happenings— not only familiar phenomena like visions, trances, and levitations; but things more marvellous, like the discovery of the elixir of life, the philosopher's stone, and the influence of the stars upon human life. Movements such as these produced their own priests, who were supposed to possess mystical powers: the fakir and the medicine man, the medium and the 'seer', the alchemist and the astrologer.

These facts should not startle us. Mystical elements have been found in all types of religion, from the most barbarous to the most refined, both in the East and West. You may trace them, for instance, in the tribal customs of savages, in the initiatory rites of the Greek and Roman 'mysteries', and in the sacramental doctrines of the higher Faiths. They are found in those great systems of philosophy, so often tinged with, and serving for, religion: Stoicism and Epicureanism, Platonism and Neoplatonism, Spinozism and Comtism: in these impressive constructions of the human spirit, mental and moral discipline are enlisted for the encouragement of the soul's growth, freedom, and vision. Often they have been found in the elaborate ritual practices of secret and semi-secret societies

of a social, political, and cultural kind; and in a variety
of sects—heretical, reforming, and even revolutionary.
A recent writer has described in a picturesque passage the
manifold forms of spiritual endeavour embraced by the
word 'mysticism': 'What possible call can collect into
one flock such diverse manifestations of the human spirit
as Neoplatonic philosophers, German pietists, Nature
poets, the great Catholic mystic saints, the alchemists and
Rosicrucians, disciples of Hindu bhakta and students of
Hindu philosophy, spiritists, Quaker and other followers of the Inner Light, the "Cambridge Platonists",
modern theosophists, the Cabalists, and ancient mystery
initiates?'[1]

That heterogeneous list, long and curious though it is,
could have been considerably extended. Mysticism, in its
range and ramifications, reminds one of Carlyle's description of the Tree of Igdrasil, the Tree of Existence, with its
roots spreading throughout the nether-kingdoms, its trunk
reaching up to heaven, and its boughs stretching over the
world.[2] Mysticism is like that: it is found in all ages and
all lands. Its roots penetrate the dark under-world of
man's hidden nature—the *unconscious*; from thence arises
the undying effort of man—the reaching up to heaven—
to discover and enjoy the abiding One; the forms of that
effort can be traced—like the branches of a tree—in every
part of the world. As we understand it, Christian mysticism represents the most fruitful bough of the Tree; and,
if it is not too fanciful, we should connect it with the
Root of Jesse.[3]

At what point then in history are we to look for the
origin of Christian mysticism? Is there any particular
gateway through which we can see it emerge into human
experience? We say there is. It is our contention that it
springs from the heart of the Gospel itself. Some critics

---

[1] Mary Anita Ewer's *A Survey of Mystical Symbolism*, p. 15.
[2] *Heroes and Hero Worship*, Lect. 1.   [3] Rom. xv. 12.

deny this, especially if they have a strong antipathy to this movement. Dr. Heiler, a most industrious investigator and a charming writer, is one of the latest of these. In his notable book, *Prayer*, he says: 'Mysticism is neither a Christian inheritance nor a peculiarity of the Christian religion, although in this religion it has assumed its finest and most beautiful form. It has penetrated into Christianity (as also into Judaism and Islam) from the outside, from the syncretist mystery religions, later religious philosophy, and especially Neoplatonism. The Gnostics and the Alexandrians, but above all Augustine and the Areopagite, were the gates by which it entered.'[1] This is a common charge: that mysticism came into the Christian religion from the *outside*. Such a view seems wilfully blind to certain elements *within* the Church from the very start. We emphasize this, because, if in our investigations we found that in the preparation for the Gospel, in the Gospel itself, and in the Church that sprang from the Gospel, there were no clear traces of mystical teaching and experience, we should seriously doubt whether we had any right to speak of *Christian* mysticism at all. Here, in these early stages, it is true, we have it only in its incipient form; but we do claim that it contains the promise and potency of the richer and fuller development. We pass the evidence in rapid review.

The Jews were not entirely without a mystical tradition. Heiler admits this, but he says it came from foreign sources. He does not indicate when and where. Most of us recognize that Jewish religion was modified by contact with Babylonian thought, and it was further affected in a later age by the all-pervading Hellenistic culture. But long before those times, great Hebrew leaders like Abraham, Moses, and Samuel had not been lacking in mystical insights and promptings. When we come to the age of the Prophets, that remarkable line of men that came in

[1] p. 170.

with the eighth century B.C., we are in the mid-stream of a vital and dynamic movement. Here were men, not only of divinely-inspired intelligence, but who in their character embodied the highest spiritual ideals. They report as something normal their extraordinary psychical experiences—auditions, visions, and revelations—all free from excess, and dubious associations. May we not also say that in the mystical utterances of their contemporaries and successors, the poets and psalmists, we catch the deep spiritual tones of the typical Hebrew faith, rather than the echoes of an alien religion? These traditions were carried on in the Wisdom literature of the Maccabean age right up to the dawn of the Christian era, and were the common inheritance of our Lord and His personal followers—the first Christian community. This long and deep stream of indigenous Hebrew mysticism is completely ignored by Dr. Heiler, and those who share his point of view.

But, a more serious omission, they totally ignore the New Testament. Why they should is a mystery. In the Gospels we have a record of the words and experiences of our Lord. His characteristic teaching is to be found in the Synoptics—the Sermon on the Mount, the parables, the instructions to His disciples—these unfailingly stress the inwardness of religion: the genuine mystical accent. Moreover, the Synoptic writers give but a mere matter-of-fact account of what at the time must have been thrilling experiences, when, in an exalted mood, their Leader lifted the veil of the future to give fleeting glimpses of the wonders to be; as, for example, when He said, 'Where two or three are gathered together in My name there am I in the midst of them',[1] the promise of the Real Presence, basis of all mystical fellowship. Do not the bare records of other outstanding events in our Lord's life—the Baptism, Temptation, Transfiguration, and Gethsemane—

[1] Matt. xviii. 20; see also Matt. xxviii. 20.

mask profound mystical experiences? From earliest times
the Fourth Gospel has been known as the 'spiritual' Gospel; it contains all the great words of mysticism; in every
age lovers of the devout life have nourished their souls in
its pages. Amongst the mystics, Paul is a master spirit.
Though he tries to write with soberness of the profound
psychical changes which came to him, and of the heavenly
manifestations he enjoyed, yet he cannot restrain his pen,
and he communicates to us something of his own rapture
as he attempts to relate what can never be told; his writings
too—especially in relation to the soul, the sacraments, and
the Church—are a treasure-house of mystical doctrine.
Miss Underhill's book, *The Mystic Way*, is devoted to a
study of the mysticism of the New Testament; in the
Preface she says she expressly wrote the work to prove that
the Christian mystic has definite qualities which differentiate him from mystics who have been evolved along
other lines, Oriental, Neoplatonic, and Mohammedan.
She claims that this differentiation is acknowledged by
such independent investigators as Leuba and Delacroix,
and she sums up: 'All the experiences characteristic of
genuine Christian mysticism can be found in the New
Testament; and I believe that its emergence as a definite
type of spiritual life coincides with the emergence of
Christianity itself in the Person of its Founder.'[1]

Through the efforts of the Early Church the Gospel
sped with incredible swiftness along the highways and into
the byways of the Roman Empire. Before the end of the
first century, its heralds had invaded the chief cultural and
commercial centres of that cosmopolitan world. Wherever
it went, it never failed to elicit in some hearers its own
particular response, the soul's glad apprehension of God.
It produced a series of men, movements, and writings
which astonished that clever and cynical age. Men of
indomitable faith like Ignatius, who, on his way to

[1] p. vii.

martyrdom at Rome, could write with burning pen, 'My Love is crucified and there is no room in me for another love'. [1] Irrepressible movements of the Spirit like Montanism, which showed how free, spontaneous, and quickening was the Divine Life, and how incapable of being confined in set forms and rigid formulae. Writings of indisputable charm and power like the Epistle to Diognetus, where Christians are described as 'this new race of men', and it is affirmed that, 'what the soul is in the body, Christians are in the world'. [2] In every part of the Early Church you feel the pulse of joyous Life: it indicates the presence of the mystical stream.

If the above considerations have convinced us that Christian mysticism is a genuine child of the Gospel, it is now necessary for us to go further; we must next examine the charge that it was really an offspring of the Graeco-Roman world, and that it actually came to birth in Alexandria. What basis is there for such an assertion?

It will be appreciated that when Christianity adventured forth into that strange and teeming world it ran tremendous risks. Was it to be expected that in all places it would retain its pristine simplicity? It was to encounter vastly different races, with dissimilar forms of thought, speech, conduct, and worship: how would it stand the shock? We can see what happened at Alexandria, though we must always remember that similar forces were at work in many parts of the Mediterranean world.

Alexandria was a great and splendid city. After the decline of Athens it had become the intellectual capital of the ancient world. It stood at the junction of East and West. Its busy streets were thronged with traders and scholars of all nations. Whilst it was proud of its commerce, its chief interest was culture—often allied to deep spiritual yearnings. Rival systems of philosophy and religion sprang up like mushrooms, and passed as quickly

[1] Ep. to Rom., vii.   [2] Radford's edition, pp. 52, 66.

away. Two of the more enduring claim our attention. *Gnosticism* was syncretistic: i.e. it strove to combine what it regarded as the best elements in Greek philosophy, Hebrew religion, Oriental speculation, and Christianity; thus equipped, it tried to give a satisfying account of the Unity behind phenomena, and to explain the relationship between eternity and time, spirit and matter, good and evil, Christ (as an emanation from the Divine) and man. Sometimes it ran to absurd excesses. *Neoplatonism* was of nobler mould. As its name indicates, it claimed to base itself on the doctrines of Plato and his School. Many of its aims were the same as Gnosticism, and it was influenced not a little by that movement; but it worked on a higher intellectual plane, and in a clearer spiritual atmosphere. Of special interest to us, it believed that man possessed a faculty, by the exercise of which he could pass behind the phenomenal world, and gain intuitive knowledge of the Absolute; under certain rare conditions this would lead to ecstasy. In harmony with this belief, the Neoplatonists evolved a technique—'a ladder of ascent'—by which the soul could be trained to climb to God. Perhaps it will now be clear why some one has said that 'Neoplatonism served as a nurse of Christian mysticism'. I would underline the word nurse; Neoplatonism was not the parent.

This brings us to two of the most significant figures in the history of Christian mysticism, both of whom underwent preparation for their life's work in the schools of Neoplatonism: Augustine, and Dionysius the Areopagite.

Augustine (A.D. 354–430) is one of the most commanding personalities of the past. He has been called the Father of Christian theology; but he was so successful a pioneer in a number of important spheres that he became a parent of many things. What he learned from Neoplatonism—and what subsequently he had to unlearn—he tells with poignant frankness in his *Confessions*, that peerless story of a soul's search for God: a search that

ended in the discovery of Christ. Salvation through
Christ was the supreme factor in Augustine's conversion;
it was equally supreme in his adaptations of Neoplatonic
teaching to Christian needs. We see this in the way he
lifted 'the ladder of ascent' out of the school of philosophy,
and set it in the Temple of Christ, where it became 'The
Scale of Perfection'.[1]   Augustine christianized Neoplatonism; which is a different thing from neoplatonizing
Christianity. Hence, 'St. Augustine's Christianity, when
at last he attained it, was the complete and vital Christian
mysticism of Paul'.[2]

Although Dionysius the Areopagite (c. A.D. 500) holds
a unique place in the development of Christian mysticism,
he is an enigma. 'The true name of this author is unknown. He was probably a monk, possibly a bishop, certainly an ecclesiastic of some sort; his home is believed
to have been Syria.'[3] He must have been a man of
immense intellectual force. Had he not been preceded by
others—notably Plotinus—his bold flights into the metaphysical stratosphere would have filled us with wonder.
As it is, when we try to follow him, he takes away our
breath, and makes us dizzy. 'The basis of his teaching is
the Super-Essential Godhead.'[4] This Godhead is 'beyond'
everything: beyond spirit, matter, and form; beyond
thought, imagination, and feeling; beyond everything we
can conceive: He is the super-transcendent Deity, the
Hidden Dark. Yet there is a twofold mode of approach.
The *affirmative way* is 'progression downwards', through
ranks of celestial beings, created things, and the nature
of man; because all these in some way participate in the
Super-Essence, they give partial manifestations of Him.
We have to make the most we can of these 'reflections':

[1] See *Confessions*, Bk. VII, Ch. xvii, Bigg's edn.
[2] *The Mystic Way*, p. 299. For a comprehensive summary of Augustine's
teaching, see Przywara's *An Augustine Synthesis*.
[3] C. E. Rolt's *Dionysius the Areopagite*, p. 1.
[4] Rolt, p. 4.

'holy crumbs which fall from the Divine table'.[1] The *negative way*, most favoured by Dionysius, is 'progression upwards', and is really a process of self-annihilation, stripping the mind of all its contents and processes: 'like as men who, carving a statue out of marble, remove all the impediments that hinder the clear perceptive of the latent image and by this mere removal display the hidden statue itself in its hidden beauty', so we strip off all 'qualities' in order that 'we may begin to see that Super-essential Darkness which is hidden by all the light that is in existent things'.[2] The reward is *union* with the super-essential Ray of divine Darkness; and the fruit of this union is ecstasy: the Beatific Vision.

However much we may feel—and perhaps deplore—the difference between this heady speculation and the simplicity of the primitive Gospel, there is one thing we must admire: that is, this man's amazing skill in his effort to transfer the whole intellectual outfit of Neoplatonism—its metaphysics, terminology, and psychological methods—to the Christian religion, in order to equip that religion for its task of winning the world for Christ, especially the Graeco-Roman world of that age. For such was the object of this remarkable monk-philosopher: to exalt Christ. Dionysius completed the work of Augustine; and both followed Paul's example in his attitude to the Mosaic Law: they strove to make Greek Philosophy a 'schoolmaster' to bring men to Christ.

In order to get a complete, as well as a clear, mental picture of what happened to Christian mysticism in Egypt, it is necessary to glance at another movement which sprang up in that land. I refer to Monasticism. As early as the second century, not a few Christians, driven out by persecution, were living in dens and caves of the desert; but others retired to these solitudes voluntarily.

[1] Dr. Rufus Jones's *Studies in Mystical Religion*, p. 108.
[2] Rolt, pp. 195–6.

They wanted to avoid the perils of the world. On the one hand, there were pleasures, luxuries, and dissipations which, through their appeal to the senses, constantly enticed them to moral ruin; on the other, there was the wild and reckless spirit of speculation which could quickly lead them to intellectual chaos, and ultimately to unbelief. Eager souls thought it safer to flee from the world to some isolated place, where without temptation or distraction they could give themselves to the cultivation of the spiritual life. These were the hermits or anchorites. As their fame for sanctity spread they soon had many imitators. One of the first and most famous of these desert-dwellers was Anthony (A.D. 251–356). He lived in absolute solitude, and practised the most rigorous asceticism; to read of his austerities is painful. His favourite disciple, Macarius, took a far-reaching step. As the number of hermits rapidly increased, he determined to organize them into 'lauras', or communities. This was the origin of Christian Monasticism.

Under Macarius the monastic life was systematized. All who entered a community had to take the triple vow of poverty, chastity, and obedience; they had to promise to devote themselves exclusively to spiritual exercises like reading, prayer, meditation, and contemplation; and they had to observe rules of discipline—based upon a thorough knowledge of psychological laws—to ensure the soul's steady advance to its goal: 'the beauty of holiness'. By this means it was expected that the initiates' growth in sanctity would follow an orderly and well-defined pathway—'the scale of perfection': first purgation, the cleansing from sin; next illumination, the coming of spiritual graces; and then union, the soul's conscious fellowship with the Divine, leading on to ecstasy. Corresponding to these three stages the brethren were classified as beginners, proficients, and perfects. No one would deny that the monastics owed something to Oriental ideas and customs, and to Neoplatonic teaching and practice; but they claimed the authority of the New Testament writers for their whole mode of life, more especially the teaching of our Lord upon self-surrender, self-control, and self-denial.

From this brief account of Egypt's twin movements, Neoplatonism and Monasticism, we may be better able to judge her contribution to the Church's mystical theology. Each of these movements had much in common, and each easily coalesced with the other. It might be no misstatement to say that Monasticism was, in part, the practical application of Neoplatonic principles. From this double source arose the system which entered into the Christian cloister, and through that institution exercised, for a thousand years, an enormous influence upon the Church's life, teaching, and practice. We may regret this. We may think too big a price was paid. It is not difficult to set down a list of debit items. Some most frequently alleged are: that it was too drastic a departure from the simplicity and naïve enthusiasm of the Early Church; that it substituted cold abstractions like the Absolute, the Divine Dark, and the Desert of the Godhead, for our Lord's conception of the Heavenly Father; that its almost exclusive emphasis upon the *negative way* offended and injured human personality, especially in its three central functions of thought, feeling, and volition; that its rigorous asceticism dishonoured and undermined the powers of the body; that its cultivation of the ecstatic state tended to induce psycho-physical phenomena like semi-hypnotic states, trances, and delusions; and that its elevation of celibacy led to a wrong attitude towards the necessary institutions of marriage, home, and the family. On the other hand, we must not forget the credit side of the account. A few of its items will readily occur to most of us: its provision, for that and subsequent ages, of a metaphysical background for the soul's questions and questings; its rich and flexible vocabulary; its psychological charts and drill; its service to scholarship—particularly literature, art, medicine, and the sciences; its ever-ready help for the poor, the sick, and the neglected; its production of heroic types of personality; and most of all, its illustrious lines of saints, whose worth and work for the Church and world are beyond compute.[1]

The point I wish to stress, however, is that in these seemingly risky and gigantic experiments the Christian religion was not sacrificing itself to powerful competitive forces; rather it was subduing them to its own purposes. By ways like these it sought to fulfil its mission, 'Go ye therefore and *make disciples* of all nations'.[2] When it encountered apparently intractable material it did not quit the field; with incredible spirit it attacked the alien mass, and either mastered or destroyed it. There may be more in this than meets the eye. Although it happened centuries ago, only in our day are some of the fruits of victory becoming visible. People of the East are learning with a shock of surprise that the Christian Faith offers them deeper and more lasting satisfaction than their own ancient beliefs. Mohammedans, Buddhists, Brahmins, and Hindus are making glad discoveries. The Sadhu Sundar Singh is a portent. 'The mystic East' is finding it easy to come to Christ because of those doors opened in Egypt long ago. As a matter of fact, what we have been watching is only part of a much larger effort. In other spheres the Church had to show the same selective skill. She was without polity: she took it from Roman law and government. She was without architecture: she appropriated the best that Rome and Greece could offer. She had no theology: she accepted help from Greek philosophy, notably in the elaboration of her creeds. In all this the Church did not lose her identity. Instead, she showed she was alive: a vital organism, with marvellous

---

[1] See H. A. L. Fisher's *A History of Europe*, pp. 250–2.
[2] Matt. xxviii. 19, R.V.

powers of selection, adaptation, and expansion, thrusting out into ever-widening circles of human thought, activity, and service. The conflict we have traced in Egypt was a section of this triumphant movement. That is why we claim it as a victory for the Church's Founder. Christian mysticism sprang from the heart of Christ. That was the gateway through which it emerged into history.

But if there is still a lingering doubt as to the origin of Christian mysticism, it is only necessary to mention a further important fact in order to dispel it. There is an influential school of investigators who emphasize the claim that there is another type of mysticism entirely indepen-dent of Neoplatonic influence to which they give the name of 'Western Mysticism'. They say that it existed from the beginning of Christian experience, and they trace it through certain of the hermits represented in the writings of Cassian, and later through Augustine, Gregory, and Bernard. Dom Butler wrote his book, *Western Mysticism*, in proof of this thesis. He summarizes it as '. . . a type of mysticism with clearly marked characteristics that differentiate it from other types of mysticism, earlier or later. It may be described as pre-Dionysian, pre-scholastic, and non-philosophical: unaccompanied by psycho-physical concomitants, whether rapture or trance, or any quasi-hypnotic symptoms; without imaginative visions, auditions, or revelations; and without thought of the Devil. It is a mysticism purely and solely religious, objective and empirical; being merely, on the practical side, the endeavour of the soul to mount to God in prayer and seek union with Him and surrender itself wholly to His love; and on the theoretical side, just the endeavour to describe the first-hand experience of the personal relations between the soul and God in contemplation and union'.[1]

This careful writer admits that Augustine's ideas and language are, in a measure, coloured by Neoplatonism;

[1] pp. 187–8.

but he claims that Cassian's teaching is quite identical with Gregory's and Bernard's.

It was this type that held sway in many Christian communities of the West from the sixth to the twelfth centuries. After that the Dionysian began to prevail. This was given considerable help by the use St. Thomas Aquinas made of its teachings in his Scholasticism. But its appeal was widened much more by the practices and writings of famous mystics like the Germans, Eckhart, Tauler, and Suso; the Fleming, Ruysbroek; and the Spaniards, St. Teresa, and St. John of the Cross. These, with their circles, gave the monk-philosopher's message an all-pervading influence in Europe. But the Western type was not crushed out. In many places it had struck deep roots. This was true of England. Here it found congenial soil. It suited our temperament. When we come to deal with the English Mystics, we shall find that the author of *The Cloud of Unknowing* showed some preference for Dionysius, but that the rest of the group favoured this more moderate type. In them there are no more than echoes of the Dionysian teaching.

CHAPTER II

THE TIMES OF THE ENGLISH MYSTICS

THIS brief historical sketch aspires to be nothing more than a background to the following studies. It seeks to focus attention on the chief events and relevant factors only of the later Middle Ages. It is hoped that it will enable readers to visualize more clearly the ecclesiastical and national setting of the individual mystics—the texture in which they had to weave their pattern of personal holiness. This will not only help to a truer appreciation of their life and witness, but it will also provide a clue to the interpretation of their teaching and message. More than this, even a short review of the age in which these saints lived cannot but increase our marvel at the serenity and beauty of their lives. We sometimes complain about the religious difficulties of our days; as compared with the conditions faced by the English mystics, we shall see how little cause there is for self-pity.

Because this Island has always been intimately linked with the Continent it has shared in the great movements originating there. This was just as true for the Middle Ages as for to-day. Not only was this country part of the Catholic Church, but it participated in the politics, culture, trade, and wars of the Continent. Hence we must first take a glance at Europe.

In its periodic explosive outbursts Europe resembles a volcano. Age after age it has rumbled, flared up, and erupted, scattering its destructive and death-dealing lava all around. Its most recent exhibition was in 1914–18;

though there have been numerous mutterings and threatening flashes since then. It was playing the same un-
pleasant game in the age we have to consider. During
the thirteenth and fourteenth centuries Europe was in a
state of almost constant eruption. From end to end it
was red with the fires of wars, rebellions, and persecutions;
and from these glowing craters there poured forth streams
of havoc and slaughter, sweeping over fruitful country-
sides and fair cities, leaving only desolation and silence.
This was specially true of the Western half of the Continent, within the confines of what was proudly called the
Holy Roman Empire, and which claimed to be the lineal
descendant of the empire of the Caesars. The Eastern
Roman Empire, whose magnificent capital, Constanti-
nople, rivalled Rome itself, was regarded as a usurper.
Between these two empires there was constant strife. But
the main and most serious struggle was in the Western
Empire, between the papacy and the monarchy. Suc-
ceeding popes and emperors were ceaselessly at death
grips. The pope was striving to make the emperor
subordinate to himself, and to rid the Church of secular
control. The emperor was equally determined to maintain his absolute independence, and not to relinquish any
of his authority in ecclesiastical affairs. 'It was the
most striking phase of the perpetual contest, which runs
through all history, between the spiritual and temporal
powers, between Church and State, between authority
which rests on persuasion and authority which rests on
force.'[1] Within this larger framework there were other
incessant conflicts. Emperors fought rival emperors, and
popes resisted anti-popes. As though these antagonisms
were not enough, bitter feuds were carried on amongst
kings, princes, dukes, and nobles; and frequent insurrec-
tions broke out amongst the peoples. For generations
Europe was stricken with the curse of war; the volcano

[1] Prof. A. J. Grant's *A History of Europe,* p. 264.

was practically persistently active; devastation and death came to be the accepted order of things. In such an age the agonies of the common people can well be imagined. They find poignant expression in the pages of the writers of those days—the chroniclers, poets, and mystics.

In the early days of the wider struggle between the papacy and the monarchy, the pope more often than not was successful. He possessed invisible but potent arms in the use of which he became a past-master. The terrors of ex-communication; the greater terrors of the anathema, which cut off the offender from intercourse with his fellow men; and the interdict, which deprived a whole community of the means of grace: these were the dreaded weapons of the papacy.[1] The rulers of the earth, and the common people, could never forget what happened to Henry VI at Canossa, to Frederick Barbarossa at Venice, and to Con-radin, the last of the 'viper brood' of the Hohenstaufen at Naples. 'The papacy triumphed, but to secure that triumph it had used weapons which were more disgrace-ful, and in the long run more ruinous, to its power, than defeat could have been. The highest motives of religion, the supremest spiritual powers in the hands of the pope, had been prostituted to personal and ambitious ends. . . .'[2]

The triumph of the papacy in the execution of Con-radin (1268), was followed in less than thirty years by the most severe defeat it received in all its career. This was administered by the kings of France. After many years of internal strife the kingdom of France had become united. It had acquired large territories, had annexed many rich cities, possessed well-trained and disciplined armies, and was conscious of its own power. At such a time the pope—Boniface VIII, crowned 1294—rather unwisely chose to challenge the authority of the royal house of France. It led to immediate disaster. The pope, as usual, hurled his

[1] See Dr. G. P. Fisher's *History of the Christian Church*, p. 231.
[2] Grant, pp. 295-6.

spiritual thunderbolts, but they fell harmlessly to the ground. He wildly called upon all and sundry to come to his rescue: there was no response. No one respected him; no one feared him. 'None was so poor as to do him reverence.' In the speedy decline of the papacy, three steps can be marked. First, the 'Babylonish Captivity' (1309–78), during which the popes lived with all the style of worldly monarchs at the luxurious and vicious court of Avignon; but they were practically the vassals of the French king. Second, the 'Great Schism' (1378–1417), when a succession of rival popes was elected; not until two or three general councils of the Church had tried to heal the breach was the scandal removed. Third, a progressive debasement in the character of the popes: this achieved its foulest type in the infamous Roderigo Borgia, Pope Alexander VI (1492); amongst his crimes were perjury, poisoning, robbery, simony, and immorality. That men so vile could occupy the chair of St. Peter, brought that exalted office into contempt; never before had the papacy been regarded with such universal feelings of abhorrence.

Nevertheless, strange as it may seem, in these unpropitious times, far-reaching spiritual movements were born, and flourished. Indeed, but for these beneficent tides of quickening and renovating life, it is hard to think how the Church could have avoided collapse. There was the formation, early in the thirteenth century, of the two great mendicant Orders, the Dominicans and the Franciscans. These preaching friars, who visited every country in Europe, did much to support the popes against princes and prelates alike; they were also the relentless foes of heresy and schism. Their real work, however, was to instruct the people, and to practise charity—especially by caring for the poor, nursing the sick, and administering spiritual comfort to the dying. Later on, some of the most influential names in the history of the Church were to be found in their ranks. Every one regrets the subsequent deterioration of these Orders. Other less organized spiritual groups sprang into existence. Such, for instance, as the Beguines, societies of women who gave themselves to prayer and charitable service; and the Beghards, similar societies of men. Scholasticism must also be included amongst movements of this kind. At the peak of its influence, it was both spiritual and cultural: 'Faith seeking for knowledge' was its motto. To-day we have a better understanding, and therefore a deeper appreciation, of the Schoolmen. We can not only admire their industry and the wide range of their inquiries, but we can see that they made valuable contributions to important subjects like theology, philosophy, morals, and politics; their metaphysical and psychological speculations are still full of interest. The work of these men did much to redeem the Middle Ages from the stigma of sterility; and to make the long-accepted description, 'Dark Ages', a misnomer.

Then there were the mystics. Miss Underhill draws a striking comparison: 'In vivid contrast to the state of the official Church, with the papacy at Avignon, and sins and abuses of every kind flourishing almost unchecked, was the network of mystical devotion—mostly propagated by groups of layfolk gathered round some saintly character—which spread over Western Europe, and attracted to itself all fervent spirits. . . .'[1] These devout servants of God, while not shunning the noise and strife of the world, concentrated almost exclusively on inward religion; by so doing, they developed noble and impressive types of character which, as examples of the 'beauty of holiness', have seldom been surpassed. However, as illustrations of pure and undefiled religion, they were neither idle nor silent witnesses. Some gave themselves to teaching, preaching, and healing ministries; theirs was a consum-

[1] *The Mystics of the Church*, p. 153.

mate demonstration of the fruitfulness of the *mixed* life: a combination of *contemplative* and *active* lives. Some aimed at reform; and the spirit in which they faced all ranks and conditions of society—but especially the clergy—and condemned the prevalent corruptions and abuses, was a piece of daring to admire. St. Catherine of Sienna's courage was typical of that of many. 'She was born at a time of almost unequalled ecclesiastical degradation. We know this, not from Protestant critics, but from the terrible words in which she and other Catholic saints of the fourteenth century described the clerical corruption which they saw.'[1] Catherine did not hesitate to confront the supreme pontiff himself, Gregory XI, at Avignon, to persuade him, for the sake of the Church, to return to Rome. Where the great ones of the Church and State had failed this intrepid mystic triumphed.

Still others of these spiritual guides took to writing; their works now rank amongst the Church's devotional classics. In view of the speedy invention of the printing-press, which would turn out books in ever-increasing numbers, this fact can hardly be over-stressed. A few of the best-known authors were: in Germany, Metchthild of Magdeburg, Eckhart, Tauler, and Suso; in Flanders, Ruysbroek; in Italy, Dante, Jacopone da Todi, and Catherine of Sienna. In Germany and the Netherlands, societies sprang up calling themselves 'Friends of God'; from their circles came two of the most popular and widely read devotional works which have had an unparalleled influence: the *Theologia Germanica* and the *Imitation of Christ*. Writers were also busy in Spain, France, Scandinavia, and of course, England.

It may be difficult for us in these days to realize the close connexion that existed between this country and the

[1] Underhill, p. 152.

Continent in the later Middle Ages. We might imagine
that our much more rapid means of communication and
travel would give us a distinct advantage over the peoples
of an earlier age. Wireless has cancelled distance; and
the aeroplane has made the dwellers in Europe our next-
door neighbours. These achievements of modern science,
however, may not guarantee that we and the folk across
the Channel are really in intimate touch with each other. Is
not most of the international trouble to-day due to the
fact that, owing to our intensified—almost morbid—sense
of nationality, we are not able to share with one another
the deeper claims and concerns of our common humanity?
Mutual confession, based on mutual knowledge, would
work wonders. In the Middle Ages this dangerous irritant
had not started to invade particular groups. There was
no racial consciousness as we understand it. Europe was
one.[1] What boundaries existed were mainly feudal, and
were in a state of flux. Human conditions were nothing
like so static as we have sometimes imagined. Within the
ever-changing areas of baronies, provinces, and kingdoms,
there was a steady movement of population. This was
specially true of the ruling classes, of Church officials, and
of teachers and scholars.[2] Trade representatives took to
the road as well. Hence the people of those days, free from
our antipathies and inhibitions, could enter more completely into one another's experiences. England profited
by these exchanges.

One institution which greatly helped in the free and
active interchange both of personalities and ideas was the
Catholic Church. How Christianity came to this country
remains a problem. Sustained efforts by keen investigators to penetrate the mists of obscurity in which its origins
are veiled have proved unsuccessful. Of this, however,
we may be sure: whoever those first missionaries were,

[1] 'Internationalism is a great mark of the Middle Ages.' Grant, p. 401.
[2] See H. A. L. Fisher's *A History of Europe*, Ch. XX.

they would teach the British to regard themselves as part of the one Church of Christ. There would in fact be every reason for those early believers, conscious of their manifold needs, to cherish this wider association. Much valuable historical evidence proves that they did so. But after the withdrawal, early in the fifth century, of Rome's legions, the British Church had to face a desperate ordeal. The fierce Nordic invaders drove the native inhabitants of the Island to its western parts; in the sanguinary process they all but extirpated the Christian Faith. How long it might have survived amongst the Celtic tribesmen in the mountain fastnesses of Wales, it is impossible to say. But once again, in the time of darkest night, Christian missionaries made their appearance in this land. At the end of the sixth century, Augustine and his monks landed on the south coast; from Canterbury they began to spread the light. Soon after, in the North, a very different mission presented itself: the Celtic band of evangelists, under the saintly and intrepid Aidan, from Iona; and here, it may be, were descendants of the original British Church. Their success was wonderful. 'The ascetic yet cheerful life of these ardent, lovable, and unworldly apostles of the moorland, who tramped the heather all day to preach by the burnside at evening, won the hearts of the men of the North. Indeed, Christianity has never, since its earliest years, appeared in a more attractive guise.'[1]

Unfortunately, if any co-operation between the two missions was attempted, it did not last for long. The English soon discovered that there were acute differences between the Celtic and Roman types of Christianity. The Celtic was primarily missionary and evangelistic; that the Roman type was not lacking in these elements was evident in the coming of Augustine and his band, but it was equally clear that these elements were subordinated to

[1] Prof. G. M. Trevelyan's *History of England*, p. 60.

Rome's love of organization and authority. The English proved themselves restive under the Roman rule. Before long, sharp disputes broke out. The differences came to a head in the prolonged and bitter controversy over the time of observing Easter. After repeated failures, a final effort at settlement was made at the Conference at Whitby (A.D. 664); but this ended unsatisfactorily in an attempt to enforce peace. This the Celtic section would not accept. So, with their sympathizers, they withdrew. They were the first Nonconformists. That break was a sad omen. 'It cannot be denied that the decision of Whitby contained the seeds of all the trouble with Rome, down the ages to come.'[1] Indeed, those discussions at Whitby were both a revelation and a prophecy: they showed unmistakably the English spirit of independence, and they forecast with unhappy accuracy much of the subsequent history of the Church of Christ in this Island.

When the Normans came in the eleventh century, it did look as though the pope's grip on this country would be strengthened. The new situation created a most favourable opportunity. Between the Normans and Italy were close ties. It was to be expected that Norman ecclesiastics would come in increasing numbers, and that they would be advanced to the chief offices of the Church—those of priors and abbots, archdeacons and bishops. Two of their number, Lanfranc and Anselm, occupied the highest seat of all—Canterbury. Had the successive occupants of the throne of St. Peter been worthy of their high and holy rank, and had they attempted to administer this realm with any suggestion of Christian charity, it is possible they might have won the heart of England, and, in some modified form, the Roman type of Christian faith might have been firmly established here through the coming centuries. But the popes made no such effort. Instead, they were guilty of such oppression, provocation, and folly, as

[1] Trevelyan, p. 61.

to stifle all kindly feelings and respectful instincts in the
hearts of our countrymen. The literary records of the
period show how the decent people of this country were
shocked by the moral decline of the papacy which led to
the 'open scandal' of Avignon: the Vicar of Christ
became a title of contempt. In addition to this, England
had to endure the insatiable covetousness of the popes.
For their wars and intrigues, for their satellites and relations, and especially for their worldly manner of life, they
needed a constant supply of gold. Well-fed streams were
kept flowing from this country. By collecting the incomes
of rich livings which were kept vacant; by appointing
their own nominees who were frequently absentees; by
bargaining to receive a large percentage of the revenues
of those actually appointed; and by similar ingenious
schemes, the papacy extorted enormous sums of money.
Later, other fruitful sources were discovered: masses, pardons, and indulgences were hawked throughout the country; sometimes they were auctioned to the highest bidder,
or even staked upon a throw of the dice. These wrongs
did not pass undenounced. Men of fearless spirit, like
Stephen Langton and Robert Grosseteste, John Wycliffe
and William Langland, stirred the soul of the nation by
their stinging indictment of the avarice and duplicity of
the popes. Had the popes not been blind, they would
have seen flashing in the eyes of these men the first lightnings of the coming storm; a storm that was brewing
slowly and silently, and which, when the time came,
would break with terrific violence over the Church; but,
in the end, it would cleanse, sweeten, and quicken the
spiritual atmosphere of the whole realm.

Here is a striking passage from Trevelyan, that
not only indicates what might have been, but also
sets out, along with the evils described above,
other glaring injustices which cried aloud for reform:

'In the fourteenth and fifteenth centuries the Church refused every concession, effected no reform, and called in brute force to repress heresy. If an opposite course had been followed; if the rights of sanctuary and benefit of clergy had been modified; if ecclesiastical property had been redistributed more fairly to the poor parson; if priests had been permitted to marry their wives as in Saxon times; if the pope had ceased to job rich places of the Church for foreign favourites; if the ecclesiastical authorities had withdrawn their countenance from the sale of pardons and relics and other superstitious practices that revolted the better sort of laity, orthodox as well as heretic; if the Church courts had ceased to make a trade of·spying on the lives of the laity in order to extract fines for sin; and finally, if Lollardy had been tolerated as Dissent, there would have been religious evolution spread over several centuries, instead of the religious revolution which we know as the Reformation.'[1]

There is a sense, therefore, in which it can be claimed that the *Roman* Catholic Church was never completely rooted in this country. In many parts, the earlier and simpler type of Catholic Faith associated with Iona was preferred to the later and more highly-developed system which came through Canterbury. Many evidences of this are seen in the pages of Bede, especially in the illuminating correspondence he has preserved. The same can be said about the still more elaborate rites and ceremonies brought by the Normans from the Continent. It can readily be understood that the conquered would not be too eager to adopt the alien customs of the victors, particularly if they happened to cut across their own cherished predilections. Indeed, as you follow the fluctuating fortunes of Rome in her efforts to make her place secure, you get the impression of a forceful system striving to impose itself from without, rather than that of an acceptable fellowship warmly welcomed from within. Rome was never naturalized here.

[1] Trevelyan, p. 245.

All this goes to show that in this Island there was slowly emerging through the centuries an indigenous Church—a Church of England—within the larger Catholic body. In the early Christian centuries we see it struggling to birth in the soul of the British people. It was never to be destroyed. During the long period of freedom from external aggression secured by the Roman occupation, the infant Church had the chance to grow up; before long it could produce martyrs, scholars, and missionaries. After the departure of the Imperial legions, it had to fight hard against pagan invaders to maintain itself; not only did it succeed, but ultimately it claimed the strangers as its own children. Its debt to Continental Catholicism was immense. That would-be Mother bestowed her treasures with a lavish hand. I think not only of the great personalities she provided, or of the religious instruction she gave; I remember also what she did to advance scholarship—especially art, literature, law, and architecture. These are debts no one wants to forget. But Rome was really a Step-mother; that is why, for this English child, she had not in their fullness the true maternal instincts of understanding, insight, patience, and selfless affection. Had she possessed these requisites the story might have been different; for then she would have been more long-suffering with our idiosyncrasies, more accommodating to our inherent love of freedom, and more willing to listen to our cries of distress. Rome never got beneath our skin.

As it was, when the Nation had really grown up; when it spoke its own language; produced its own literature; evolved, through its universities, its own culture; made in its Parliament its own laws; when it laid down limits to the authority of its own King: then it was natural it should demand its own Church. The Reformation was inevitable. That much-esteemed modern historian, whom I have already quoted, has said on this point, 'Every important aspect of the English Reformation was of native origin. All can be traced back as far as Wycliffe, and some much farther'.[1] That 'much farther' covers, of course, the English mystics; they played no small part as precursors of the Reformation movement in this country.

In this historical outline we must also include some reference, however brief, to the more familiar details of daily life in the Middle Ages. Because of what has been said, let it not be too hurriedly assumed that this period was one long unrelieved spell of hopeless misery, both of body and mind. As we have seen, there were many fruitful causes of suffering. War, in one guise or another, was seldom absent; there were periodic outbursts of plague, and the constant threat of other forms of fearsome disease, like leprosy; famine, due both to drought and flood, was not uncommon; and devastating fires frequently brought ruin. Yet in spite of these terrors the people had learned some knack of extracting honey from the rock. Salzman, in a picturesque passage, presents an attractive scene:

'The closer we look at medieval England, the more we shall feel inclined to picture it as young and hardy and joyous. To begin with, the country was full of colour. The churches glowed with stained glass and painted walls; the dresses of the wealthy, men as well as women, were gorgeous and brilliant, and if the peasantry wore more serviceable russets and browns and blues, they usually managed to introduce a splash of red or other bright colour in their hoods or kerchiefs. And the country was full of song, and with this went dancing.'[2]

Other popular games and sports were horse-racing, hunting, and coursing; cock-fighting and bull-baiting, though often cruel spectacles, drew large crowds. At holiday-times there were keen competitions in running, leaping, shooting, wrestling, casting the stone; ball games and mimic tournaments were also much enjoyed. But

[1] Trevelyan, p. 250, and H. A. L. Fisher, p. 353.
[2] *English Life in the Middle Ages*, p. 24.

probably no other form of entertainment was quite so universally popular as the miracle plays. These, performed in the churches, and in the open air, were elaborately presented; and while their main design was to teach Biblical history, they also aimed at instruction and amusement. They contained a good deal of fun and humour.

All this colour, sport, and enjoyment helped to contribute to the environment of the mystics. So, too, did the more serious interests. Art was active in many branches. Architecture, for instance, was winning some of its greatest triumphs. In different parts of the land, massive Gothic cathedrals were springing up, amazing for their nobility of conception, and beauty of design: their grandeur still fills us with a sense of wonder. While painting never flourished here as in some parts of the Continent, yet there was an East Anglian school that did notable work in the cathedrals and churches. On the other hand, in the decoration of manuscripts, the skill of medieval Englishmen was unequalled; in the illumination of service books the East Anglian artists drew exquisite designs. England was likewise famous for its artistic metal work, especially in gold and silver: much of this went to the beautifying of the churches in the forms of altar ornaments, chalices and crosses, banners and images. Music, both instrumental and vocal, was popular with all classes.

Attempts had been made to systematize, and even to humanize, law, but at its best it was a savage and vindictive instrument; terrible punishments were inflicted for petty crimes. Hanging was a common penalty; and if a criminal escaped the gallows, he would probably be mutilated by having his hand or foot cut off, or blinded by having his eyes gouged out. Science, as we understand it, had hardly begun; hence the prevalence of astrology, magic, and witchcraft, with their brood of superstitions, which exercised a baleful influence over the minds of multitudes.

Such is the wide and variegated background to our studies: as we pass the mystics in review, we shall see that its lights and shadows fall upon them. That means they fit into the age in which they lived. We shall find, although they lived solitary or semi-solitary lives, they were keenly sensitive to the hopes and fears, joys and sorrows, sympathies and antagonisms which possessed the hearts of the people, and that they had their own definite angle from which to judge the facts underlying these feelings. We shall also find it of absorbing interest to watch their reactions to those mighty spiritual forces which, as we have shown, were surging through the country, pressing upon the hearts, minds, and consciences of men, demanding a verdict. We shall rejoice that the mystics did not try to evade the issue; that they had their answers to the great and agitating questions of the day; and it may be, they will surprise us by the depth and daring of their judgement, and their forward-looking vision. In addition we shall point out from time to time how these vast spiritual forces were formative factors in shaping the life, character, and message of these saints.

While it is true, however, that the mystics fit into their age, the fit is by no means perfect. We ought not to expect that it would be. Part of them escapes from that particular section of history, because they carry in their soul that which is timeless. Their essential message—that which springs from the depth of their soul—is for every age. That is why it is so pertinent to-day. As we read parts of these writings, we shall feel that they were sent out specially for us. They both correct and confirm. These medieval saints will lay their fingers on the weak and ugly places of the soul to-day: but those same fingers will also point the way to hope and sure triumph.

We shall find, too, that these mystics are *English*. That

means they not only sprang from the English Church, but that all about them they bear marks of their race— the rock whence they were hewn, the pit whence they were digged. They are independent in spirit, lovers of freedom, brave in their championship of the poor and the oppressed. They are outspoken, sometimes indiscreet. In spiritual matters they stand for simplicity, sincerity, and directness. Especially are they English in their love of the Bible, the interpretation of its truth for daily living, and in making its message available for their 'even-Christians'. English again is their urgent emphasis upon the need of cultivating personal relationships with Christ, the assurance that this open and immediate fellowship is offered to every believer, and the certainty that this fact of the soul's union with its Divine Lover is the heart of the Christian Gospel.

I must add that these are the characteristics which bring these early English mystics so close to the hearts of Free Churchmen. We feel they are our spiritual kith and kin; across the centuries, without effort, we greet them as our brothers and sisters in Christ. True, in their burning protests against the ecclesiastical vices and social evils of their day, we think we hear more than echoes of our own voices—doubtless their protests had something to do with our becoming *Protestants*. But those are not the proofs of our lineage. Our affinities are in the deeper regions of the soul. When they probe the wounds of sin in their hearts, and cry out for healing: their pain and shame are ours. When in glad humility they celebrate the Divine Grace which seeks, cleanses, and redeems them, and they bow in adoring wonder before the Cross of the Saviour: we know something of their holy rapture. When, in rare moments, they have been caught up to a flashing glimpse of the unveiled Face, and their tongue could not tell of the marvel: we have hints of that ecstasy. The soul's ever-evolving experiences of Divine Love, symbolized in their mystical terms of purgation, illumination, contemplation, and vision—these are the links between us and them. We Free Churchmen can simply avow that we have accepted these saints as our spiritual guides, because they lead us to the ever-fresh and ever-flowing springs of Eternal Life.

The above facts make it apparent that 'The Times of the English Mystics' were packed with interest and incident. Life was neither stale nor stagnant. This was true, in particular, of the fourteenth century, which, with a little extension at the beginning and end, was the actual period covered by the lives of the mystics. It might fitly be described as an Age of Awakening. The old order was disintegrating; a new was pressing in. As the new strongly urged itself forward, it threw up movements—social, cultural, religious—which played a powerful part in shaping our later national development. I shall mention only one or two of the chief.

1. There was the emancipation of the serf. Was not that the first successful blow for coming Democracy? It had three great allies. The Hundred Years' War (1337–1453) revealed that the archer with his long-bow was equal in worth as a fighter to the knight in armour: 'Jack was as good as his Master.' The fetters of feudalism were really smashed at Crecy, Poitiers, and Agincourt. The Black Death (1349) reduced the population by nearly one half; by that same ratio it enhanced the economic value of the labourer. The Peasants' Revolt (1381) showed that the masses were learning to organize, and were willing to go to desperate lengths to achieve their freedom.

2. There was the emergence of the English tongue. Since the Conquest it had hidden itself away, like a thing of shame, in obscure places; but now, by Parliamentary decree, it became the recognized language of the realm: it was heard in the law-courts, churches, schools, and the homes of all classes. It immediately sprang into diverse

forms of poetry and prose; some of enduring strength and beauty, like William Langland's *Piers Plowman* (1332–1400), *Chaucer's Tales* (1340–1400), and the *Works of John Wycliffe* (1320–84). Moreover, these first notable literary creations of our mother tongue are valuable as expressions of the hopes and fears of the best minds of that age—social reformers, scholars, and preachers—as they looked out upon the life of their times: they also enable us to hear the very voices of the fourteenth century, freely discussing the Court, government, Church, law, and social conditions generally. In this regard the writings of Wycliffe, including his translations of the Scriptures into the vernacular, are specially noteworthy. They not only mirror their age, but they were a mighty spiritual force in helping to produce a revival of religion which, carried on for another two centuries by Wycliffe's followers, the Lollards, found its consummation in the wider triumph of the Reformation.

3. Then there was the dawn of a healthy national consciousness. Some of its main causes have already been referred to: success in war, advance in language and literature, growth in representative institutions; but other agents were: the spread of trade, the observance of law, and the rise of education and knowledge. This new spirit of unity, in welding the various classes together, not only thrust out internal jealousies and hostilities, but, in its turn, had a vital influence upon such institutions as the Throne, Parliament, and the Church; Kingship and absolutism began to part company; Parliament took on more and more the form of a representative assembly; and the Church became more National—the famous Statutes of Provisors (1351) and Praemunire (1353, 1365, 1393) did much to curtail the power of the Pope, and to check his interference in the affairs of this country.

These were the stirring times in which the mystics lived. Some writers claim that three of our authors—of the

Ancren Riwle (*c.* 1225), the *Cloud* (*c.* 1350), and Dame Julian (1342–1413)—appear to have been unaffected by the events of their day. But that is as much as to say that these saints lived in a vacuum. Of course, such complete isolation of personality is impossible. Even those who try to live the solitary life are touched in innumerable ways by the spirit of their age: their mental conceptions, like their verbal expressions, will be cast in the mould of current forms. So, if we read the above authors carefully, we shall find that their lives and writings show many marks of their epoch; indeed, only by an historical approach can we properly understand and appreciate them. This is specially true of the other three authors: Richard Rolle (1290–1349), Walter Hilton (1330–96), and Margery Kempe (1373–?). The writings of these contain direct references to contemporary happenings; and only by some knowledge of the period can we fully share their ideas and feelings.

CHAPTER III

THE 'ANCREN RIWLE'

In the Middle Ages, an anchorhold or a hermitage was a common sight in this country. It might have been a hut in the woods, a cave on the moors, or a hovel in the fields. More often than not it was a chamber built on to a church. This cell would have two windows: one looking into the church to enable the recluse to take part in the religious services; the other—'the parlour window'—giving a view of the world. Sometimes these dwellings contained two rooms, or even three. This allowed the ancress to have a serving 'maiden', who protected her from intrusion and attended to her bodily needs. The outside window was the gathering place for all kinds of people who came to consult with the holy person within. An anchorite or ancress who had gained a reputation for sanctity would become an object of pilgrimage. Super-natural powers over body, mind, and soul were attributed to them; the Chronicles of the age teem with stories of their miracles.

The vow to undertake this sacred vocation was regarded as binding for life. This gave rise to many legends of virgins who were immured—'built up'—in these cells, never to leave till death set them free. The candidate for the solitary state usually received preliminary training in a nunnery. On the day she began her new life as an ancress, a solemn service of dedication was conducted by the bishop. Once she had entered her cell every earthly relationship was severed. No longer could her nearest and dearest claim her as a kinswoman; she was the spouse of Christ. Many of us might regard this as 'a living death';

to the ancress it was the reverse, 'a dying to live'. She believed that by her supreme act of renunciation, blessed by the rites of Holy Church, she had transformed a little parcel of earth into a corner of heaven: cherubim and seraphim—the angelic hosts—were now her constant companions.

The *Ancren Riwle*[1] was written for 'three pious sisters' who undertook this mode of life. Whatever age this book had come from it would have been a notable production; but springing as it did from the end of the so-called Dark Ages it is a surprising achievement. In comparing it with other religious works of the same period a competent judge has said, '. . . this is a work which, owing to its greater originality, its personal charm, and its complete sympathy with all that was good in contemporary litera-ture, stands apart by itself as the greatest prose work of the time, and as one of the most interesting of the whole Middle English period'.[2] Lovers of the devout life will assuredly regard the *Ancren Riwle* as one of the fairest gems in the entire collection of early mystical literature. Its qualities are all wholesome: simplicity, freshness, charm; humour, pathos, and enthusiasm. Sunshine streams from its pages. When it describes Divine Love it becomes lyrical. Some of its passages glow with a spiritual fervour that cannot fail to enkindle a flame in one's own soul. Naturally, it bears the birthmarks of its age. Con-stant use is made of allegorical teaching; strange and subtle analogies abound; deep and hidden meanings are found in Biblical names and terms; and now and again there is clever play upon words. The author, however, never allows his fancy to run wild, nor does he descend, like some contemporaries, to puerilities. Indeed, when he

[1] *The Ancren Riwle* (or *The Nun's Rule*), modernized by James Morton. 'The Medieval Library,' No. 18. Quotations in this chapter are from this edition.

[2] Prof. J. W. H. Atkins in *Cambridge History of English Literature*, Vol. I, p. 230.

is indulging these conceits of his times, you enjoy his quaint skill and picturesque phrasing.

Scholars are agreed that the book was produced at the beginning of the thirteenth century, when 'the motives of love and mysticism began lightly touching the literary work of the time to finer issues'.[1] It was written in the curious Anglo-Saxon of that period. Richard Poore, Bishop of Salisbury from 1217 to 1229, and founder of that city's cathedral, was for some time accepted as its author; but to-day we are not sure. Long and keen dispute has taken place on the question, and it is not yet settled. Maybe after further investigation tradition will be found to be right.[2] The bishop was said to have written the Rule for a small group of ancresses at Tarrent in Dorsetshire. The good Richard was born at this place, and at the end of a busy life he came back there to die. These facts would account for his taking a deep interest in its religious house. If we may assume the bishop's authorship, this book shows him to have been a man of delightful personality, with a keen sense of humanity, and a broad outlook upon life. One imagines he would have been equally at home in cottage or mansion, farm or school. He was familiar with the facts and processes of agriculture and industry; he could find pleasure in games and sports; and he was a lover of the wild life of the countryside. His scholarship was immense. He lays under the same easy contribution Fathers and Doctors of the Church, and philosophers and poets of Greece and Rome. Of his utter devotion to Christ, and to the duties of his episcopal office, there is abundant evidence. Altogether, he must have been a worthy and lovable character.

The *Ancren Riwle* gives many indications of the warm affection between this father-in-God and his young pupils. He constantly expresses his concern for their wel-

[1] Atkins, *Cambridge History of English Literature*, Vol. I, p. 217.
[2] See article 'Ancren Riwle' in *Encyclopaedia Britannica* (14th ed.).

fare; and he does his best to ensure it. Thus he says there are two rules: the one relates to the right conduct of the heart; the other to the regulation of the outward life. Do they ask which rule they should observe?

'Ye should by all means keep well the inward. . . . This rule is not framed by man's contrivance, but by the command of God. Therefore, it ever is and shall be the same, without mixture and without change; and all men ought ever invariably to observe it. But all men cannot, nor need they, nor ought they to keep the outward rule in the same unvaried manner. . . . No anchorite, by my advice, shall make profession, that is, vow to keep anything as commanded, except three things, that is, obedience, chastity, and constancy as to her abode. . . . I would not have you make a vow to keep external rules as a divine command; for, as often thereafter as ye might break them it would too much grieve your heart and frighten you, so that you might soon fall, which God forbid, into despair, that is, into hopelessness and distrust of your salvation.'[1]

Should any ignorant person ask them what order they belong to, they are to reply that they are of the order of St. James, who says what religion is, and what right order: 'Pure religion and undefiled before God and the Father is this, To visit the fatherless and widows in their affliction, and to keep himself unspotted from the world.'[2] The bishop's comment on this text gives a flashing glimpse into his mind:

'Herein is religion, and not in the wide hood, nor in the black, nor in the white, nor in the grey cowl.'[3]

All this is pleasant and illuminating. This wise spiritual adviser does not wish his friends to saddle themselves with useless impedimenta; that is why he tells them so explicitly to avoid man-made laws. By that same advice he lets us see where his own emphasis lies—he is all for the inner life: fellowship with Christ.

[1] pp. 3–7.   [2] Ep. of St. James i. 27.   [3] p. 9.

The writer possesses intimate details of their family life and their spiritual condition.

'For I know not any ancress that with more abundance, or more honour, hath all that is necessary to her than ye three have. . . . There is much talk of you, how gentle women you are; for your goodness and nobleness of mind beloved of many; and sisters of one father and one mother; having, in the bloom of your youth, forsaken all the pleasures of the world and become ancresses.'[1]

He tells how their needs are plentifully met by the kindness of a near-by benefactor, possibly a friend of the family:

'For ye take no thought for food or clothing, neither for yourselves nor for your maidens. Each of you hath from one friend all that she requireth; nor need that maiden seek either bread, or that which is eaten with bread, further than at his hall.'[2]

The treatise opens with an Introduction that describes the book's purpose, and outlines its contents. There follow eight parts. The work is so carefully constructed, and each part so complete in itself, that the task of presenting the author's teaching is considerably simplified.

He begins with religious duties and ceremonies; their number is astonishing. The greater portion of the day must have been taken up with a repetition of hymns, prayers, psalms, and Scripture passages. Undoubtedly these exercises might become mechanical; on the other hand, if done in the right spirit they could prepare the soul for moments of rapture. In the midst of these instructions the good bishop could write:

'After the kiss of peace in the mass, when the priest consecrates, forget there all the world, and there be entirely out of the body; there in glowing love embrace your beloved Saviour who is come down from heaven in your breast's bower, and

---

[1] pp. 144-5.   [2] p. 144.

hold Him fast until He shall have granted whatever you wish for.'[1]

That first part ends with the plea:

'I pray you never be idle, but work, or read, or be at beads, and in prayer, and thus be always doing something from which good may come. . . . In bed, as far as you can, neither do anything nor think, but sleep.'[2]

The section on 'Keeping the Heart' deals with the five senses—'the wardens of the heart'. Exponents of mysticism have long recognized the worth of this chapter as containing sound psychological teaching, and acute spiritual diagnosis. Also, the author's clever use of allegory is apparent here.

SIGHT gets heedless souls into many troubles. Eve is the standing example and warning; for sin first entered into her through her eyes:

'Wherefore, my dear sisters, love your windows as little as possible; and see they be small—the parlour's smallest and narrowest.'[3]

TASTE is treated of most fully in the last part of the book. There it is shown that the appetite must be controlled by systematic fasting. Here, the author refers to the tongue as the organ of speech, and describes the evils of much talking:

'Let not the ancress have the hen's nature. When the hen has laid, she must needs cackle. And what does she get by it? Straightway comes the chough and robs her of her eggs and devours all that of which she should have brought forth her live birds. Just so the wicked chough, the devil, beareth away from the cackling ancresses all the good they have brought forth, which ought, as birds, to have borne them up to heaven.'[4]

HEARING leads to endless temptations, and to much scandal:

'People say of ancresses that almost every one hath an old

woman to feed her ears; a prating gossip who tells her all the tales of the land; a magpie who chatters to her of every thing that she sees or hears; so that it is a common saying, "From miln and from market, from smithy and from nunnery, men bring tidings". Christ knows, this is a sad tale. . . .'[1]

SMELLING, if misused, may bring dire penalties:

'Be warned of this, my dear sisters, that sometimes the fiend maketh something to stink that ye ought to use, because he would have you avoid it; and, at other times, the deceiver maketh a sweet smell to come as if from heaven, in order that ye may think that God, on account of your holy life, sends you His grace and His comfort, and so think well of yourselves and become proud.'[2]

TOUCHING, or feeling generally, is a sense to be so jealously guarded that an ancress cannot be too careful. There must be no handling or touching, under any circumstances, between her and a man. Further,

'God knows that I would a great deal rather see you all three, my dear sisters, women most dear to me, hang on a gibbet to avoid sin, than see one of you give a single kiss to any man on earth, in the way I mean.'[3]

He has much of importance to say on the character of ancresses. In spirit, an ancress must strive to be like Christ: gentle, kind, patient, and affectionate. Anger, especially, no matter what people say or do, must at all times be avoided. A 'testy ancress' or a 'peevish recluse' does great harm.

'There are two kinds of ancresses whom our Lord speaketh of; the false and the true. "Foxes have holes, and the birds of heaven have nests." The foxes are the false ancresses. . . . The fox is a thievish and ravenous beast, and devours eagerly withal: and the false ancress draweth into her hole and devours, as the fox doth, both geese and hens; and hath, like the fox, a somewhat simple appearance, and yet is full of guile, and affecteth to be different from what she is; she is a hypocrite. . . .

[1] p. 67.   [2] p. 79.   [3] p. 87.

True ancresses are compared to birds; for they leave the earth; that is, the love of earthly things; and, through yearning of heart after heavenly things, fly upward toward heaven. . . .'[1]

Recluses ought to live so holy a life that the whole Church may lean upon them, and be supported by them:

'An ancress is for this reason called an ancress, and anchored under the church as an anchor under a ship, to hold the ship so that neither waves nor storms may overwhelm it. In like manner shall ancresses, or the anchor, hold the Holy Church Universal, which is called a ship, so firm, that the devil's storms, which are temptations, may not overwhelm it.'[2]

When dealing with carnal and spiritual temptations, he enumerates certain comforts for those assailed, and recommends helpful remedies. This chapter is specially interesting in its treatment of the seven deadly sins, which are presented under the symbolism of the wild beasts of the wilderness: 'a venerable but effective method of teaching'.[3] The wilderness is a life of solitude—of monastic or anchoretic seclusion.

'In this wilderness are many evil beasts—the lion of pride, the serpent of venomous envy, the unicorn of wrath, the bear of dead sloth, the fox of covetousness, the swine of greediness, the scorpion with the tail of stinking lechery, that is, lustfulness.'[4]

Each of these 'beasts' has a litter of 'whelps': the special vices which spring from each sin. Shrewd spiritual insight is shown in selecting and describing these vices; this is particularly true of the sin of 'accidia', which the author calls sloth. 'Accidia' was a fatal weakness in monastic life: it was the restless misery and boredom which attacked the contemplative when spiritual vision failed.

'The bear of heavy Sloth hath these whelps: Torpor is the

[1] pp. 97, 99.   [2] p. 107.
[3] *Cambridge History of English Literature*, Vol. I, p. 227.
[4] p. 148.

first; that is, a lukewarm heart, which ought to light up into a flame in the love of our Lord. The next is Pusillanimity; that is, too faint-hearted, and too reluctant withal, to undertake anything arduous in the hope of help from God, and in confidence of His grace, and not of her own strength. The third is Dullness-of-heart. Whosoever doeth good, and yet doeth it with a dead and sluggish heart, hath this whelp. The fourth whelp is Idleness; that is, any one who stands still doing no good at all. The fifth is a Grudging, grumbling Heart. The sixth is a deadly Sorrow for the loss of any worldly possession, or of a friend, or for any displeasure, except for sin only. The seventh is Negligence, either in saying, or doing, or providing, or remembering, or taking care of any thing that she hath to keep. The eighth is Despair. This last bear's whelp is the fiercest of all, for it gnaweth and wasteth the benignant kindness, and great mercy, and unlimited grace of God.'[1]

The writer is again in line with traditional mystical teaching when he describes the first years of the religious life as 'nothing but ball-play' between the Lover and the beloved. An ancress might think that she would be most strongly tempted in the first twelve months or two years; consequently she is distressed to discover that time brings no relief, instead, temptations assail more fiercely. Why is this?

'If Jesu Christ, your Spouse, doth thus to you, my dear sisters, let it not seem strange to you. For in the beginning it is only courtship, to draw you into love; but as soon as He perceives that He is on a footing of affectionate familiarity with you, He will now have less forbearance with you; but after the trial—in the end—then is great joy.'[2]

A little further on he says the same thing again, only he changes the figure of speech. In this passage we have another of the beautiful metaphors often employed by writers on the devout life.

'Our Lord, when He suffereth us to be tempted, playeth

with us, as the mother with her young darling; she flies from
him and hides herself, and lets him sit alone, and look
anxiously around, and call Dame! Dame! and weep awhile,
and then leapeth forth laughing, with outspread arms, and
embraceth and kisseth him, and wipeth his eyes.'[1]

The bishop, as a loyal son of the Church, expresses
unquestioning faith in her sacramental system; naturally,
he wishes his pupils to share his enthusiasm. He pleads
movingly for a sure trust in the miracle of the mass:

'Believe firmly that all the power of the devil melteth away
through the grace of the holy sacrament, which ye see elevated
above all, as oft as the priest saith mass, and consecrateth that
Virgin's child, Jesus, the Son of God, who sometimes de-
scendeth bodily to your inn, and humbly taketh His lodging
within you. God knoweth, she is too weak, and too evil-
hearted, who, with the aid of such a guest, fighteth not
bravely. Ye ought to believe that all that the holy church
singeth and readeth, and all her sacraments, give you spiritual
strength, but none so much as this; for it bringeth to nought
all the wiles of the devil. . . .'[2]

He says that next to the sacrament of the altar, the
sacrament of confession is most hateful to Christ's enemies.
As to its efficacy, it

'confoundeth the devil, and hacketh off his head, and dis-
perseth his forces; it washeth us from all our filthiness, and
giveth us back all our losses, and maketh us children of God'.[3]

The above points are exemplified in the history of Judith.
As to the kind of confession that shall produce these good
results, it shall be

'accusatory, bitter and sorrowful, full, candid, frequent,
speedy, humble, with shame, anxious, hopeful, prudent, true,
voluntary, spontaneous, steadfast, and premeditated'.[4]

Next he treats of penance. The sweet reasonableness
of the author is most apparent here—especially remembering the age in which he lived. The self-macerations of

[1] p. 174.   [2] pp. 200–1.   [3] p. 225.   [4] p. 229.

some saints, in seeking conquest of the body, make repugnant reading. This spiritual director will have none of these excesses. He begs his friends to avoid extremes. Let them practise such methods only as will keep both body and soul fit and strong.

'All that I have said concerning the mortification of the flesh is not for you, who, upon some occasions, suffer more than I could wish, but it is for some who will give this advice readily enough, who nevertheless handleth herself too softly.'[1]

He bids them endure any hardness willingly, and turn even the minor annoyances of life, to their spiritual profit. With a smile, he says:

'And be glad in your heart if ye suffer insolence from Slurry, the cook's boy, who washeth dishes in the kitchen.'[2]

In the section on Love—Christ's love of us, and our love of Him—we have some of the writer's most moving appeals. Never was the mystical experience—union with God, appropriation of Divine Life, and fulness of heavenly joy—more attractively presented. How strong, condescending, and patient is our Lord's love of us:

'There was a lady who was besieged by her foes within an earthen castle, and all her land destroyed, and herself quite poor. The love of a powerful king was, however, fixed on her with such boundless affection, that to solicit her he sent his ambassadors, one after another, and often many together, and sent her jewels both many and fair, and supplies of victuals, and the aid of his noble army to keep her castle. She received them all as a careless creature, that was so hard-hearted that he could never get any nearer to her love. What wouldest thou more? He came at last himself and showed her his fair face, as one who was of all men the most beautiful to behold; and spoke most sweetly and such pleasant words; that they might have raised the dead from death to life. . . . All this availed nothing.'[3]

Why is our response so cold?

[1] pp. 286-7.   [2] p. 287.   [3] pp. 294-5.

'Set a price upon thy love. Thou shalt not say so much that I will not give thee for thy love much more. . . . Heart shall never think of such great felicity, that I will not give more for thy love, immeasurably, and infinitely more.'[1]

Then, like all good evangelicals, he bases his final appeal on the Cross:

'Look often upon the Cross. Think whether you ought not joyfully to love the King of Glory, who so stretches out His arms towards you, and bows down His head as if to offer you a kiss.'[2]

The concluding part of this medieval treatise, giving external rules of conduct for the guidance of these ancresses, is most valuable, because it preserves so many interesting details of the domestic life of an anchorhold. The author advises the sisters to take holy communion only fifteen times a year; they are to fast moderately— never on bread and water, except they have leave; their meals must be taken at home, and no banquetings are to be provided for friends. Let them avoid Martha's part— that of housewifery; they are to imitate Mary, who chose 'the better part'—that of quietness and rest from the world's din. Ancresses must live on alms as frugally as they can; not wishful to be rich, or known as bountiful, or eager to possess. From a man they should take nothing, 'not so much as a race of ginger'. They shall not keep any beast—'only a cat': probably for keeping mice down. Otherwise, 'the ancress must think of cow's fodder, and of herdsman's hire, flatter the hayward, defend herself when her cattle is shut up in the pinfold, and moreover pay the damage'.[3] They should not take charge of other people's property, not even the church vestments, or the chalice. No man is to sleep within their walls; if in case of necessity a house should have to be so used, 'have therein with you a woman of unspotted life day and night'.

[1] p. 302.   [2] p. 305.   [3] p. 316.

Their clothes may be white or black, as long as they are plain and warm—skins well tawed; 'and have as many as you need, for bed and back'. They are to wear no iron, haircloth, or hedgehog skins; they must not beat themselves with a scourge of leather thongs, nor must they, without leave of their confessor, cause themselves to bleed with holly or briars. Shoes must be thick and warm. They are to have neither ring, broach, ornamented girdle, nor gloves.

As to their works: 'Make no purses, to gain friends therewith, nor blodbendes[1] of silk; but shape, and sew, and mend church vestments, and poor people's clothes.'[2]

An ancress must not become a schoolmistress; her maid may teach any little girl who might not be able to learn among boys. They shall have their hair cut four times a year, and their blood let as often. 'Wash yourselves wheresoever it is necessary, as often as ye please.'

An ancress whose food is not at hand may employ two women: one who stays always at home, another, plain and of sufficient age, who goes out when necessary. They must be obedient to their dames, avoid men, never sleep out, never bring or carry idle tales, and hate lying and ribaldry. In appearance and dress, behaviour and possessions, they must copy the example of their mistresses. They must never quarrel. An ancress must give constant oversight in all these matters; she is responsible for the material and spiritual well-being of her servants; it is a solemn trust for which she will have to give an account to the Supreme Judge.

The treatise ends on a very human note:

'In this book read every day; for I hope it will be very beneficial to you, through the grace of God, or else I shall have ill employed much of my time. God knows, it would be more agreeable to me to set out on a journey to Rome, than

---

[1] Bandages for stopping bleeding.   [2] p. 318.

to begin to do it again. . . . As often as ye read any thing in this book, greet the Lady with an Ave Mary for him who made this rule, and for him who wrote it, and took pains about it. Moderate enough I am, who ask so little.'[1]

We shall gratefully acknowledge that this manual is a peerless guide to the religious life of the Middle Ages; but, before leaving it, a word must be said about another eminent feature: the many vivid glimpses it gives of the general life of the times—of the people, their customs, interests, pastimes, and daily concerns.

For instance, you see the leech, with his many boxes full of electuaries and phials; the professional beggars, 'crafty varlets', who cover their good clothes with torn smock-frocks, and expose their ulcers and sores to excite the pity of the rich; the trumpeters, who blow a loud blast of music to proclaim the presence of their lords; the jesters, who, to provoke mirth, make wry faces, distort their mouth, and scowl with their eyes; the knife-throwers, who play with swords and hold them on their tongue by the sharp point; the wrestler, with his many cunning tricks to throw his opponent; and the play performed in the churchyard.

Just as interesting are the author's references to the farm and field: to the thievish fox, full of guile; to the wild boar that cannot stoop to smite him who falls down; to the 'tristre', the place where men wait with greyhounds to intercept the game, or to prepare nets for them; to the 'cubbel' tied to the swine that is too much given to ranging and raking about; to the foolish purchaser, who, when he is about to buy a horse or an ox, will look only at the head; to the man who immediately beats the dog that gnaws leather or worries sheep, that the animal may understand for what he is beaten; and to the farmer who fences young trees round with thorns, lest beasts should bite them while they are tender.

[1] pp. 325–6.

In this fascinating pageant of life, which moves in and out of the writer's pages, we frequently catch sight of priests and friars, monks and nuns. The conduct of these religious classes was a stock subject of conversation amongst all ranks of society. Their vanities and indiscretions would add spice to table and tavern talk; their darker failures would provide endless themes for scandal and gossip. In dealing with certain types of clerics our author himself can be very candid and caustic.

'A feeble man comes forward and esteems himself highly if he have a wide hood and a close cope, and would see young ancresses, and must needs look, as if he were of stone, how their fairness pleases him. . . . Believe secular men little, religious still less. . . . Confession of secret sins ought to be always prudent, and made to a prudent man, and not to young priests, I mean young of wit, nor yet to foolish old men. . . . An ancress may confess to any priest such open sins as all men are liable to fall into; but she must be well assured and confident of the integrity of the priest to whom she sheweth unreservedly how it stands with her in regard to carnal temptations. . . .'[1]

This brings us to one of the most difficult problems of that age, and of later ages: the vow of perpetual chastity. That many who took that oath proved unequal to its fulfilment is clear from this book. The only shadows on its pages are those cast by the sin of lechery. Our author, otherwise so forbearing and considerate, lashes this evil with all his might. The mere possibility of falling a victim to this vice must have haunted the solitary like a nightmare. There is room for only a brief quotation:

'The Scorpion of Lechery—that is, of lustfulness—hath such a progeny, that it doth not become a modest mouth to name the names of them; for the name alone might offend all modest ears, and defile all clean hearts. . . . For, howsoever it is done, willingly and awake, with the satisfaction of the

---

[1] pp. 44 ff.

flesh, except in wedlock only, it is a deadly sin. In youth extraordinary follies are committed: let her who feeleth herself guilty belch it out in confession, utterly as she committed it; otherwise she is condemned, through that foul flame, to the everlasting fire of hell.'[1]

Instances of the writer's skilful use of allegory, analogy, and word-play will be found in the above extracts. In conclusion, here are one or two further samples of this rare gift of figurative speech, and scintillating phrase: On the effects of a bad example:

'O dear young recluse, often does a right skilful smith forge a full weak knife.'[2]

On the necessity of preserving silence:

'But many keep in their words to let more out, as men do water at the mill-dam.'[3]

Against untruthfulness:

'She who moveth her tongue in lying, maketh of her tongue a cradle to the devil's child, and rocketh it diligently as a nurse.'[4]

On God's chastening:

'If the chalice could speak, which was molten in the fire, and made to boil vehemently, and then, with much beating and polishing, made into so very beautiful a form for the service of God, would it curse the purifying fire and the hands of its artificer? The whole world is God's smithy, in which He forgeth His elect. Wouldst thou that God had no fire in His smithy, nor bellows, nor hammers?'[5]

On humility:

'Many have a way of speaking of their sins, that it is equivalent to a covert boasting and hunting after praise of greater sanctity.'[6]

Against idleness:

'Iron that lieth still soon gathereth rust; and water that is not stirred soon stinketh.'[7]

[1] p. 153.   [2] p. 42.   [3] p. 56.   [4] p. 63.   [5] p. 214.   [6] p. 249.   [7] p. 319.

CHAPTER IV

RICHARD ROLLE

HISTORY plays curious pranks. In the middle of the four-teenth century, Richard Rolle of Hampole was one of our most prolific writers, in verse and prose, on religious subjects. During his lifetime, and for some years after his death, alike in England and upon the Continent, his numerous works were eagerly sought and frequently copied. Unfortunately, after enjoying this blaze of popularity, he was banished to the night of neglect. Why he suffered this eclipse is a mystery. It may be that during the century of political disturbances and prolonged wars, through which this country passed soon after his decease, his name simply faded out of remembrance. Or, later still, his writings may have been swamped by the spate of literature released by the printing-press at the time of the Renaissance and the Reformation. Whatever the cause, the fact remains that the incomparable works of this saint and poet all but disappeared. At the dawn of the present century his name was hardly known outside a small circle of medieval scholars. In history books he was barely mentioned, and in anthologies seldom quoted. All this has recently changed. Owing to the present revival of interest in mysticism, diligent search has been made for the long-lost manuscripts of this Yorkshire recluse, with gratifying results. His writings, to meet a widespread demand, are being reproduced in a variety of forms.

This newer knowledge is leading to a revised estimate of the Hermit. Expert authorities, after a critical examination of his works, and a careful endeavour to measure his influence upon the movements of his age, are of the opinion that he is a figure of some importance. He is fast becoming recognized as one of the main creative forces in the earlier development of our national literature and religion.

Undeniable claims for an original place of this kind can be advanced for Rolle. He was one of the earliest writers, after the Conquest, to express himself in the mother-tongue. Scholars agree that his distinctive style of Middle English—terse, incisive, graphic—has exercised no small influence on the written form of our language. Some give him the title, Father of English prose. He was one of the first to translate parts of the Scriptures into the ver-nacular. Wycliffe made use of these renderings. Hence these two Yorkshiremen share the honour of being pioneers in the making of the English Bible. Rolle will always be of exceptional interest to students of our national religion —especially if they are lovers of the devout life—because he is one of the first of the English mystics whose writings we possess. How a figure of such dimensions could have fallen into comparative oblivion is a riddle of history.

This saintly hermit is certainly a most attractive per-sonality. His candour and simplicity charm you. With-out the faintest trace of self-consciousness, he opens to you the secret places of his soul. In his larger works, where the autobiographical element is most marked, his confes-sions at times are so intimate that you get the impression you are talking face to face with your closest friend. This frankness wins you.

In this, as in many other ways, he often reminds you of the Saint of Assisi. The parallel is irresistible. Richard, like Francis, was a born romanticist: his behaviour, private and public, was characterized by unexpected and daring elements, pregnant with delightful surprise—not the way of the prudent and discreet for him! Like Francis, too, he was a gay troubadour of the Spirit: when prose failed his ecstasy, he burst into lyric song; melody was his normal form of prayer. But not only did his soul wing its way to God on outbursts of praise, his life amongst men was also set to music: it was so sunny and care-free. Again like Francis, when he stepped out of the old world into the new, he symbolized the change by an act of stripping; off came his old clothes, and with a youth's ingenuity, he fashioned some new—an imitation of a hermit's habit. This curious costume was likewise intended to be a symbol—a badge of willing servitude: for still like the 'little poor man' of Assisi, he was going to serve his Lord in poverty, chastity, and obedience.

In addition to all this, as we turn the pages of Rolle's books, we soon learn that we are under the guidance of a scholar. We are first conscious of this because of the ease and culture of his style; but evidence is also there in his references to, and his ideas and phrases taken from, Fathers and Doctors of the Church like St. Augustine, St. Bernard, Richard of St. Victor, and St. Bonaventura.

For knowledge of the outward events of his life we are dependent upon the Lessons prepared for inclusion in the Office intended to be used after his canonization. This honour was never conferred, possibly because of the tension between the English Crown and the Papacy at that period; and also because, soon after his decease, his name became associated with Lollardy. The Lessons were drawn up shortly after his death—probably by the Cistercian nuns of Hampole, to whom he was spiritual adviser. While a strain of legend runs through the story, investigation has proved that the distinctly biographical parts are in the main trustworthy.

For the much more important facts of his inner life we turn to his own works. These, written in Latin and English, were many and varied. They range from the highest class of devotional writings in prose and poetry, through commentaries on the Scriptures and the Creeds,

to practical treatises and popular tracts. For our purpose
we shall chiefly consult two collections of his prose: *The
Fire of Love and the Mending of Life*, translated from the
Latin in 1434–5, by Richard Misyn, and modernized by
Frances M. M. Comper; and *Selected Works of Richard
Rolle*, transcribed by G. C. Heseltine, containing all his
English writings, except his long translation and commen-
tary on the Psalter.[1]

We learn from the Lessons that Richard was born at
Thornton, near Pickering, in Yorkshire; no date is given,
but other authorities give a choice of two, 1290 and 1300.
His parents, judging from their social connexions, belonged
to the well-to-do classes. No particulars are given any-
where about his early life; the only information available
is the little to be gleaned from his writings. In one place
he cries out:

'Lord God, have mercy on me! My youth was fond; my
childhood vain; my young age unclean. But now Lord Jesu
my heart is enflamed with Thy holy love and my reins are
changed; and my soul will not touch for bitterness what before
was my food: and my affections are now such that I hate
nothing but sin.'[2]

In his beautiful little treatise, *Of the Virtues of the Holy
Name of Jesus*, he breaks forth:

'I went about, covetous of riches, and I found not Jesus.
I ran in wantonness of the flesh, and I found not Jesus. I sat
in companies of worldly mirth, and I found not Jesus. In all
these I sought Jesus, but I found Him not. For He let me
know by His grace that He is not found in the land of softly
living. Therefore I turned another way, and I ran about in
poverty, and I found Jesus, poorly born into the world, laid
in a crib and lapped in cloths. I wandered in the suffering
of weariness, and I found Jesus weary in the way, tormented

---

[1] An exhaustive list of Rolle's works has been prepared by Miss Hope Emily
Allen: *Writings ascribed to Richard Rolle, Hermit of Hampole*. For his poetry
readers may consult *The Life and Lyrics of Richard Rolle*, by Frances M. M.
Comper.

[2] *Fire of Love*, Bk. I, Ch. 12.

with hunger, thirst and cold, filled with reproofs and blame. I sat by myself alone, fleeing the vanities of the world, and I found Jesus in the desert, fasting on the mountain, praying alone. I went the way of pain and penance, and I found Jesus bound, scourged, given gall to drink, nailed to the Cross, hanging on the Cross, and dying on the Cross.'[1]

We must not accept too literally Richard's severe strictures upon his youth. He is regarding his past from the sun-lit heights of sanctity; from those shining summits his early days might well look dark and vain. When a young man, he was sent to Oxford by the help of Master Thomas de Neville, Archdeacon of Durham. Oxford, at that time one of the most famous seats of learning in Europe, was visited by scholars from all parts of the Continent; yet we can easily believe that the youthful Richard did not settle there with much enthusiasm. Although Scholasticism was past its prime, and its end was being hastened by William of Occam's persistent blows, it still retained the semblance of its age-long supremacy. Its method and spirit in its declining days would repel Richard; his warm heart and romantic nature would crave for something less bleak and arid. This makes it not improbable that he did, as some suggest, cross to France to complete his studies. For his residence at the Sorbonne evidence is not lacking. Be this as it may, at the age of nineteen he determined to be done with schools and universities, and even with home and friends; he was ready to take a fateful step. This should not surprise us. Adolescence is a time of instability and readjustment; more often than not it shapes the path of the future. Most young men, did we but realize it, in their pitiable confusion and craving for guidance, are 'not far from the Kingdom'.[2] Given Richard's ardent temperament, we may assume that during his growth into manhood, he would pass through times of mental stress

---

[1] *Selected Works*, p. 85.
[2] On this point Bede Frost has useful advice to spiritual directors: *Art of Mental Prayer*, pp. 225–6.

and spiritual conflict, in which he would alternate between hope and fear, faith and doubt. The crisis—like most crises—would warm up gradually, simmering in the depths of his soul. Suddenly it sprang into consciousness. With him it would have the severity of an earthquake. He faced the upheaval manfully. He would flee from the embrace of the world to the arms of God. The story of the Lessons is here dramatic and absorbing:

'He said one day to his sister, "My beloved sister, thou hast two tunics which I greatly covet, one white and the other grey. Therefore I ask thee if thou wilt kindly give them to me, and bring them me to-morrow to the wood near by, together with my father's rain-hood. . . ." When he had received them he straightway cut off the sleeves from the grey tunic and the buttons from the white, and as best he could he fitted the sleeves to the white tunic, so that they might in some manner be suited to his purpose. Then he took off his own clothes, with which he was clad, and put on his sister's white tunic next his skin, but the grey, with the sleeves cut out, he put on over it, and put his arms through the holes which had been cut; and he covered his head with the rain-hood aforesaid, so that thus in some measure, as far as was then in his power, he might present a certain likeness to a hermit. But when his sister saw this she was astounded and cried, "My brother is mad! My brother is mad!"'[1]

Soon after, on the vigil of the Assumption, he entered a church to pray—possibly at Topcliffe, near Ripon. He occupied the place of a certain lady, the wife of a squire, John de Walton. Her servants wished to remove him, but she would not consent. At the close of the service, the lady's sons recognized Richard as a fellow-student at Oxford. On the day of the feast, without asking permission, he put on a surplice and sang matins and the office of mass with the others. Then, having secured the priest's blessing, he went into the pulpit and preached a sermon

[1] *Fire of Love*, p. xlvi.

of such conviction and power that his hearers were brought to tears.

The squire was warmly attached to Richard's father as a friend, so he invited the young man to his home. After dinner he had an earnest talk with him in private. When the squire had convinced himself of Richard's serious purpose, he did a generous thing: he provided him not only with a habit suitable for a hermit, but also with food and lodging. The youth was now able to satisfy his heart's desire—to give himself to the full rigours of a recluse's life. He moved into a small cell, slept on a hard bench, and gave himself up to fasts, vigils, and frequent penitential acts.[1]

Richard was now firmly started on his life's adventure. He never looked back. With iron will he went forward in pursuit of his ideal—the achievement of sanctity. After living for some years in the vicinity of Sir John de Walton's home, and having attained a high degree of holiness, he had become a centre of interest and attraction. One day some visitors came and found him busily writing. They asked him for a word of exhortation. The good man spoke to them for two hours, yet he continued at the same time to write as quickly as before. On another occasion, he was so absorbed in prayer, that when a worn cloak was removed from him, stitched and replaced, he knew nothing about it. He had become so skilful in the use of his tongue and pen, that hearts were comforted by his words—especially his written ones:

'Yet wonderful and beyond measure useful was the work of this saintly man in holy exhortations, whereby he converted many to God, and in his sweet writings, both treatises and little books composed for the edification of his neighbours, which all sound like sweetest music in the hearts of the devout.'[2]

By this time he was ready for wider fields of activity.

[1] *Fire of Love*, pp. xlviii and xlix.   [2] Ibid., p. xlix.

He moved about from place to place, seeking by turns service and solitude. Wherever he went, many were blessed. He gave light to those in spiritual darkness, and relieved such as suffered mental or physical distress. His journeyings brought him to Richmondshire, where he became the friend and helper of Dame Margaret Kirkby, a recluse of Anderby. A mutually profitable fellowship sprang up between them. The ancress seems thoroughly to have understood the hermit. On occasions when he was wounded by vicious tongues, Margaret was able to tranquillize his sensitive spirit. Some of his books were written for this fellow-seeker after the higher life.

His last move was to Hampole, near Doncaster. In between his times of devotions and writing, he gave his services to a convent of Cistercian nuns. Here he passed away in 1349. He appears to have been a victim of the Black Death. He gave his life in saving others: that is what we should have expected.

Richard's advance in the spiritual life is easy to trace because he describes its stages, in their nature and duration, with exactness. Reference has been made to his conversion. Though it had the violence of an earthquake, it did but herald the pilgrim's start; he now describes his progress on the way:

'And in process of time great profit in ghostly joy was given to me. Forsooth three years, except three or four months, were run from the beginning of the change of my life and mind, to the opening of the heavenly door; so that, the Face being shown, the eyes of the heart might behold and see by what way they might seek my Love, and unto Him continually desire. The door forsooth yet biding open, nearly a year passed until the time in which the heat of everlasting love was verily felt in my heart. I was sitting forsooth in a chapel, and whiles I was mickle delighted with sweetness of prayer or meditation, suddenly I felt within me a merry and unknown heat. But first I wavered, for a long time doubting what it could be. I was expert that it was not from a creature but from my Maker, because I found it grow hotter and more glad. Truly in this unhoped for, sensible, and sweet-smelling heat, half a year, three months and some weeks ran out, until the inshedding and receiving of this heavenly and ghostly sound; the which belongs to the songs of everlasting praise and the sweetness of the unseen melody. . .

'Whiles truly I sat in this same chapel, and in the night before supper, as I could, I sang psalms, I beheld above me the noise as it were of readers, or rather singers. Whiles also I took heed praying to heaven with my whole desire, suddenly, I wot not in what manner, I felt in me the noise of song, and received the most liking heavenly melody which dwelt with me in my mind. For my thought was forsooth changed to continual song of mirth, and I had as it were praises in my meditation, and in my prayers and psalm saying I uttered the same sound, and henceforth, for plenteousness of inward sweetness, I burst out singing what before I said, but forsooth privily, because alone before my Maker. . . .

'Wherefore from the beginning of my changed soul unto the high degree of Christ's love, the which, God granting I was able to attain—in which degree I might sing God's praise with joyful song—I was four years and about three months.'[1]

That is a celebrated passage in the literature of English mysticism. We value it for its delightful simplicity of style and spirit, and for its illuminating description of the profound mystical changes which this dauntless seeker after the perfect life underwent. Students of mysticism point out how these changes correspond to the three stages of the mystic way: purgation, illumination, and union. It is highly probable that the Saint's advancement did reproduce these stages. Most readers, however, will prefer to interpret the passage as a poet's effort to express—as far as words will—his glad and progressive apprehension of Divine Reality.

It will be observed that Rolle describes his experiences in terms of *heat*, *song*, and *sweetness*. This he does consistently. He does not wish us to understand the words in a

[1] *Fire of Love*, Book 1, Ch. 15.

fanciful, or a merely figurative sense. For instance, when writing of *heat*, he assures us repeatedly that the term describes exactly what he feels 'truly, and not in imagination'. Lest any one should think he is suffering from illusions, he soberly writes in the Prologue of his book:

'I was forsooth amazed as the burning in my soul burst up, and of an unwont solace; ofttimes, because of my ignorance of such healthful abundance, I have groped my breast seeking whether this burning were from any bodily cause outwardly. But when I knew that it was only kindled inwardly from a ghostly cause, and that this burning was nought of fleshly love or concupiscence, in this I conceived it was the gift of my Maker.'[1]

So far as we know, Rolle was the first and last of the mystics to use this trilogy of terms. Many mystics, to express their heart's feelings when kindled by Divine Love, have employed one or another of these words; and with them, each of the three words meant much the same thing —the terms were interchangeable. Rolle never actually defines the words, but he uses each one to represent a different phase of his spiritual experience. *Heat* stands for the conscious inflowing of heavenly love. *Song* for the pouring forth of his adoring soul in gratitude to the Beloved. *Sweetness*, the state of inward joy which results from this fellowship:

'Whence truly in these three that are tokens of the most perfect love, the highest perfection of Christian religion without all doubt is found; and I have now, Jesu granting, received these three after the littleness of my capacity. Nevertheless I dare not make myself even to the saints that have shone in them, for they peradventure have received them more perfectly. Yet I shall be busy in virtue that I may more burningly love, more sweetly sing, and more plenteously feel the sweetness of love. . . .'[2]

What Rolle, with his keen sense of humour, would have

---

[1] Ibid., Prologue, p. 11.   [2] Ibid., Book I, Ch. 14.

said of some of our explanations of his ecstasies, might have
been interesting to hear. Here is one by Miss Underhill:
'Those interior states or moods to which, by the natural
method of comparison that governs all descriptive speech,
the self gives such sense-names as these of "Heat, Sweetness, and Song", react in many mystics upon the bodily
state. Psycho-sensorial parallelisms are set up. The well-
known phenomenon of stigmatization, occurring in certain hypersensitive temperaments as the result of deep
meditation upon the Passion of Christ, is perhaps the best
clue by which we can come to understand how such a
term as "the fire of love" has attained a double significance for mystical psychology.'[1]

Such descriptions of the machinery underlying the
Saint's raptures should not be taken too seriously. A smile
is a simple thing, and can be described in terms of mental
and muscular movements; but how inadequate is the
explanation. The essential element in a smile is personality; of this, psycho-physical accompaniments tell us
nothing. So here. 'Psycho-sensorial parallelisms' is a
phrase covering a network of mysteries. It says little of
real enlightenment. Concerning the method of the
Divine Spirit's operation upon our spirit it leaves us very
much where we were. On this point, Dr. Thouless says,
'It is impossible to pretend that our knowledge of psychological laws is so complete that we can honestly say that
it provides us with an explanation of the desires, thoughts,
feelings, &c., of anybody'.[2]

Rolle freely admits the mystery, and at the same time
regretfully confesses that words are useless to express the
wonder of his experiences:

'The smallness of my mind certain knows not how to open
that which as a blabberer, I am busy to show. Yet I am compelled to say somewhat, although it is unable to be spoken,

[1] *Fire of Love*, Introduction, p. xv.
[2] *An Introduction to the Psychology of Religion*, p. 261.

that hearers or readers may study to follow it; finding that all love of the fairest and loveliest worldly thing in comparison to God's love, is sorrow and wretchedness.'

'This delight, certain, which he has tasted in loving Jesu, passes all wit and feeling. Truly I can not tell a little point of this joy, for who can tell an untold heat? Who lay bare an infinite sweetness? Certain if I could speak of this joy unable to be told, it seems to me as if I should teem[1] the sea by drops, and spar[2] it all in a little hole of the earth.'[3]

What are the conditions of this love? They are stated very simply:

'Truly affluence of this everlasting love comes not to me in idleness, nor might I feel this ghostly heat while I was weary because of bodily travel, or truly immoderately occupied with worldly mirth, or else given without measure to disputation; but I have felt myself truly in such things wax cold, until, putting a-back all things in which I might outwardly be occupied, I have striven to be only in the sight of my Saviour and to dwell in full inward burning.'[4]

Lest we think these conditions too simple, he states them again in a manner that would not be acceptable to many in his day:

'Alas, for shame! An old wife is more expert in God's love, and less in worldly pleasure, than the great divine, whose study is vain. For why? For vanity he studies, that he may appear glorious and so be known, and may get rents and dignities: the which is worthy to be held a fool, and not wise.'[5]

Of those who have merely book knowledge, and pride themselves upon their learning and skill, he is not a little scornful:

'But those taught by knowledge gotten, not inshed, and puffed up with folded arguments, in this are disdainful: saying, Where learned he? Who read to him? For they trow not that the lovers of endless love might be taught by their inward

[1] empty.   [2] bolt.   [3] *Fire of Love*, Book II, Chs. 10 and 4.
[4] Ibid., Prologue, pp. 12–13.   [5] Ibid., Book I, Ch. 5.

master to speak better than they taught of men, that have studied at all times for vain honours.'

'Thou needest not covet greatly many books. Keep love in thine heart and work, and thou hast all that we may say or write. For the fullness of the law is charity; on that hangs all.'[1]

In many places, Rolle, like most mystical writers, refers to the degrees of love. On such occasions he is emphasizing the fact that love is always growing; it never stops or stagnates; upwards and onwards it constantly climbs towards the Ideal. The fullest and finest exposition of some of the stages through which it passes is in the charming eighth chapter of *The Form of Living*.

'Three degrees of love I shall tell thee, for I would that thou might win to the highest. The first degree is called *Insuperable*, the second *Inseparable*, and the third *Singular*.

'Thy love is *Insuperable* when nothing that is contrary to God's love overcomes it, but it is stalwart against all temptations and stable whether thou be in ease or anguish, in health or sickness. So that thou thinkest that thou wouldest not, for all the world and to have it for ever, at any time make God wrath. . . .'

'Thy love is *Inseparable* when all thy heart and thy thought and thy might are so wholly, so entirely and so perfectly fastened, set, and established in Jesus Christ, that thy thought goes never from Him, except sleeping. . . .'

'The third degree is highest and most wondrous to win. That is called *Singular*, for it has no peer. Singular love is when all comfort and solace are closed out of thy heart but that of Jesus Christ alone. It seeks no other joy. . . .'[2]

He often warns those who would rise highest that they must work hardest:

'The soul goes up into this height whiles, soaring by excess, it is taken up above itself, and heaven being open to the eye of the mind, it offers privy things to be beheld. But first truly it behoves to be exercised busily, and for not a few years, in

[1] *Fire of Love*, Book II, Ch. 3, and *Selected Works*, 'The Form of Living', Ch. 9.
[2] *Selected Works*, Ch. 8.

praying and meditating, scarcely taking the needs of the body, so that it may be burning in fulfilling these; and, all feigning being cast out, it should not slacken day and night to seek and know God's love.'[1]

He has no doubt about the superiority of the contemplative life over the active. He does not rush to this conclusion hastily; he carefully balances one against the other and then decides:

'By some truly it is doubted which life is more meedful and better: contemplative or active. It seems to not a few that active is meedfuller because of the many deeds and preachings that it uses. But these err unknowingly, for they know not the virtue of contemplative. Yet there are many active better than some contemplative; but the best contemplative are higher than the best active.

'Truly if any man might get both lives, that is to say contemplative and active, and keep and fulfil them, he were full great; that he might fulfil bodily service, and nevertheless feel the heavenly sound in himself, and be melted in singing into the joy of heavenly love. I wot not if ever any mortal man had this. To me it seems impossible that both should be together.'[2]

At times, however, his references to those of active life are tinged with contempt; especially if once they were contemplatives:

'This manner of man forsooth that is taken up to so high love, ought to be chosen neither to office nor outward prelacy; nor to be called to any secular errand. . . . Holy contemplatives are most rare and therefore most dear. . . . Those who will polish such, that is to say honour them with dignities, are busy to lessen their heat, and in a manner to make their fairness and their clearness dim; for truly if they get the honour of principality, they shall forsooth be made fouler and of less meed. Therefore they shall be left to take heed to their studies, that their clearness may increase.'[3]

[1] *Fire of Love*, Book II, Ch. 2.   [2] Ibid., Book I, Ch. 21.
[3] Ibid., Book I, Ch. 14.

From passages such as these—and there are many sprinkled throughout his works—it is plain that the hermit had but little respect either for the Church dignitaries of his day, or for those who made the most pious professions: 'the religious'. Of some of these latter—monks and friars who had become degenerate and greedily preyed upon rich and poor alike—he writes in his *Commentaries* with biting scorn:

'Here we pray not to live a worldly life . . .; nor to despoil the people and gather their goods into our castles, nor by the craft of flattery to please the world; but even to live the contrary life. . . . For by wandering in such ways men may well see whose children they are and for whom they make ready. For the king of all such children of pride, who is Antichrist, leads such religious and teaches them these deceits. Wherefore some men say that they are dead corpses gathered from their sepulchres, wrapped in the clothes of grief and driven by the devil to draw men. And thus they wear the badges of hypocrisy. It were less harmful to men of Christ's school to deal with a legion of the fiends of hell than with a little convent of such quick devils. For some they rob and some they make mad, and by feigned hypocrisy and the deceits of the devil they beguile more men than do other fiends. May the Lord deliver His folk from the perils of these false friars. . . .'[1]

Of still another class, whose violent deeds and cruel deceptions were the terror and shame of that age, he writes with equal vehemence. No modern reformer could have commanded more fiery invective:

'But the mighty men and worldly rich that ever hungrily burn in getting possessions of others, and by their goods and riches grow in earthly greatness and worldly power—buying with little money what, after this passing substance, was of great value—or have received in the service of kings or great lords great gifts, without meed, that they might have delights and lusts with honours: let them hear not me but Saint Job:

[1] *Selected Works*, 'Song of Zachary', p. 218.

"Their days they led in pleasure, and to hell they fall in a point. . . ".[1]

'Also here is forbidden trickery of weight or count, or of measure, or through usury, or violence or fear—as beadles or foresters do and ministers of the king—or through extortion, as lords do.'[2]

No man could write or speak so trenchantly and hope to escape reprisals. Those attacked returned with no less spirit to the charge. They gave Richard a bad time. Repeatedly he cries out because of his 'enemies'. These complaints reveal to us one of the sorest troubles of his life: he was acutely sensitive. Any act or word of un-kindness—especially from those he trusted—cut him to the quick. In many places he bitterly laments the un-faithfulness of certain friends—'scorpions', 'backbiters' —and deplores his consequent disappointment and loneli-ness.

Like all men of his class this hermit had a horror of lechery. To account for this it is not necessary to resort to the Freudian technique. Richard was as healthy-minded as any normal man. In expressing himself as he did, his intention was to maintain and enforce the traditional ideals of purity. Hence on many of his pages—particu-larly in *The Fire of Love*—you find passages such as this:

'Whiles a man weds not for pure love of God and virtue and chastity, but is busy to live in chastity and in array of all virtue, doubtless he gets to himself a great name in heaven; for as he ceases not to love God here, so in heaven he shall never cease from his praising. Wedlock soothly is good in itself; but when men constrain themselves under the band of matrimony for the fulfilling of their lust, they turn forsooth good into ill, and whereby they wean to profit, thereof they cease not to be worse.'[3]

So he warns would-be contemplatives against the

[1] *Fire of Love*, Book I, Ch. 30.
[2] *Selected Works*, 'On the Ten Commandments', p. 77.
[3] *Fire of Love*, Book I, Ch. 24.

'sweet words of fair women'. He is also impatient with the extreme freakishness of feminine fashions. We have heard similar denunciations in our own days; they remind us that while times change, things remain much the same:

'Next the women of our time are worthy of reproof that in such marvellous vanity have found new array for head and body, and have brought it in, so that they put beholders to dread and wonder. Not only against the sentence of the apostle in gold and dressing of the hair, in pride and wantonness, they go serving; but also against the honesty of man and nature ordained by God, they set broad horns upon their heads, and horrible greatness of wrought hair that grew not there, some of whom study to hide their foulness or increase their beauty and with painting of beguiling adultery they colour and whiten their faces.'[1]

Lest any one should think, because of these fulminations, that Richard was the slave of an anti-feminine complex, it should be pointed out that several contemporary writers deplore the vanity, slackness, and infidelity of certain classes of women. These vices were attributed, in no small degree, to the interference of the friars in domestic relationships. This became a serious menace, and produced endless trouble. Of course, Richard knew the value of good women, and handsomely acknowledges his debt to them.[2] The deep and abiding friendship, wherein he found true solace of soul, between him and Margaret, shows his real attitude towards women; so, too, did his spiritual labours for the nuns at Hampole.

Some of Rolle's characteristics will commend—it may be endear—him, to many in our day. We cannot but admire his fine spirit of independence. It is specially creditable in those days, and undoubtedly had important historical consequences. It comes out in such a simple act as his sitting for devotions: though frequently reproved for this by 'fond men', he quietly went on his own way.[3]

---

[1] *Fire of Love*, Book II, Ch. 9.   [2] Ibid., Book I, Ch. 12.
[3] Ibid., Book II, Ch. 1.

We readily admit that a man of that temperament is not easy to control, or even to persuade; and doubtless he would be a thorn in the flesh of many, most of all, of those Church authorities who might try to curb him, and fasten him down to orthodox ways. The same spirit is seen in the following passage, where he is writing upon *The Creed of Athanasius*: here he distinctly reminds us of later Protestants:

'This psalm tells us much of the Trinity, but it is not necessary for every man here to know it, since a man may be saved if he believes in God and hopes that God will teach him afterwards what is necessary. . . . For our creed should be mixed with love and faith, so that faith may teach our reason how good God is. . . . So love and good living are necessary to a right faith. But God forbid that men believe that every man who will be saved must believe expressly every word that is said here, for few or none are in that state, either Greeks or Latins. And yet, even for us, English fails to express what little we believe. For faith is of truth, which is before our languages. And, as we say, God gives faith both to children and to men although they have not the power to learn faith of their brethren.'[1]

His freedom of thought is also apparent in his attitude towards the ecclesiastical system of his times. While he recognizes that such practices as fasting, confession, penance, and regular attendance at mass are good as discipline and spiritual helps, he nowhere presses them as being necessary to salvation. His writings are markedly free from references to transubstantiation. He gives a more Protestant emphasis still when he says:

'The name of God is taken in vain in many ways. With heart, false Christian men take it in vain who receive the Sacrament without grace in the soul.'[2]

On the other hand, he never tires of stressing the constant necessity of prayer, meditation upon the Scriptures,

[1] *Selected Works*, p. 225.
[2] Ibid., 'The Ten Commandments', p. 76.

and 'the practice of the Presence of God'. Then, as he often gratefully acknowledges, his personal devotion to the Saviour is the centre of his spiritual life: a fact that comes out most clearly in his choice little work, *The Amending of Life*. All this may be summed up by saying that Rolle stands for experimental religion as distinct from ecclesiastical, institutional, or sacramental. That is why I find it difficult to agree with Dom David Knowles when he says, 'His temperament and outlook were unusual, but he was neither an innovator, nor a reformer'.[1] I think he partook of both.

One is bound to refer to the vein of humour running through Richard's works: a dry broad humour—he was a Yorkshireman. On many a page you see the hermit's homely smile, especially when he is giving your folly or vanity a gentle rub. He often administers raps like this:

'How mayest thou for shame, who art but a servant, with many clothes and rich, follow thy Spouse and thy Lord, who went in a kirtle; and thou dost trail as much behind thee as all that He had on.'[2]

His works abound in deep, pithy, paradoxical sayings, expressed in clear and incisive speech, which make an indelible impression on the mind. Here is a short catena on Love:

'What is love but the transforming of desire into the thing loved?'

'Therefore if our love be pure and perfect, whatever our heart loves it is God.'

'But, know it well, he himself knows not love that presumes to despise common nature in his brother; for he does wrong to his own condition that knows not his right in another.'

'Such truly as we now are to Him, such a one shall He then appear to us; to a lover certain lovely and desirable, and to them that loved not, hateful and cruel.'

[1] *The English Mystics*, pp. 86–7.
[2] *Selected Works*, 'The Commandment', p. 7.

'Hate thou no wretchedness on earth except that that thy
pure love can cast over and disturb; for perfect love is strong
as death, true love is hard as hell.'[1]

Enough has now been said to suggest something of the
true lineaments of this Saint. Richard Rolle was a great
man—of that there can be no doubt. Look at the men
whose work he foreshadowed, it may be, directly influenced: Langland, who voiced the sufferings and needs of
the common people; Chaucer, often referred to as the
creator of English literature; and Wycliffe, the precursor
of the Reformation. From these men sprang prevailing
movements, whose seeds were in the heart of Richard
Rolle. But Richard's real greatness was in himself, in
those essential qualities which mark him as a born mystic:
his devotion to the spiritual life, his achievement of holiness, his joy of fellowship with the Beloved, and his care
for the friendless, the afflicted, and the perplexed. These
are the authentic unveilings of Richard's inner nature:
they win our love, and find full expression in 'his sweet
writings, both treatises and little books, which all sound
like sweetest music in the hearts of the devout'.

[1] *The Fire of Love*, Book I, Chs. 17, 19, 25; Book II, Chs. 8, 11.

CHAPTER V

'THE CLOUD OF UNKNOWING'

HERE we meet another of history's teasing tricks. Competent judges agree that *The Cloud of Unknowing*, with its slender sheaf of tracts,[1] is one of the most valuable groups of devotional writings to be found in any religious literature. Yet concerning the author every essential detail of biography is lacking: his name, date, birth-place, condition of life, contemporaries and friends—not a hint of any of these has come down to us. The only fact for which there is any evidence is that he lived in the fourteenth century; and that is a deduction from a comparison of his writings with other works of the period whose date is known. What makes the entire absence of these biographical details the more surprising is that there are indications that this author's books were popular and had a wide circulation. A tangible piece of information of this kind is the large number of early manuscripts of his works which have survived, and the excellent state of their text. In his day he must have been a notable character. That the name and reputation of this successful spiritual guide—undoubtedly one of the most interesting personalities in the long line of English mystics—should have faded into complete obscurity is one of the minor tragedies of history.

[1] Seven books in all are attributed to this author: *The Cloud of Unknowing*, *The Epistle of Privy Counsel*, *Denis Hid Divinity*, *Benjamin*, *The Epistle of Prayer*, *The Epistle of Discretion*, and *Of Discerning of Spirits*. The first three of these are contained in *The Cloud of Unknowing, And other Treatises*, by Dom Justin McCann; and the other four in Edmund G. Gardner's *The Cell of Self-Knowledge*.

Fortunately, however, we are not left entirely in the dark as to the kind of man he was. If historical facts are denied us, we have some compensation in the many important details of the writer's character to be gleaned from his productions. These books are so charged with their author's spirit as to convey a definite impression of his personality. He was a man of strong individuality. In disposition he was generous and genial, though at times the sunny landscape of his life could cloud over, and its shining serenity be broken by the rush of a passing storm. His mind was acute and vigorous: his penetrative intellect could sound the depths of metaphysical speculation, and his keen imagination was undaunted before the loftiest ranges of spiritual adventure. His sure touch in dissecting mental processes and tracing them to their roots marks him an expert psychologist. His humour—quaint, subtle, shrewd—was delightful; as occasion arose he could exercise a playful fancy, or a mordant wit. Considering that he wrote when English was still passing through its infancy, his command over our mother tongue is astonishing: his force, fluency, and pungency of style are a constant surprise. Most of all, he had a distinctive religious experience—of the contemplative order—which gave colour, tone, and strength to all his compositions. Gifts and qualities of this kind must have made our author not only a spiritual genius, but also a charming friend.

Many guesses as to who this writer was have been made. Towards the end of the fifteenth century he was identified with Walter Hilton; but that idea has long been abandoned. Other suggested names have met a similar fate. All that the latest editor, after a careful study of the writings can say is that 'he pictures him as a University man—Cambridge is perhaps more likely than Oxford— who became incumbent in a parish in East Anglia, and there pursued the study and practice of the contemplative life'.[1] This judgement will not gain universal assent, as not a few investigators have proved to their own satisfaction that the author was a monastic—possibly a Carthusian. For this last contention—that he was a religious —I confess to feeling some partiality. Perhaps it is best, till further evidence is forthcoming, to regard the problem as insoluble.[2]

When we discuss the reason for the composition of these treatises we are on firmer ground. The author repeatedly affirms that he prepared them for the use of aspirants to the contemplative life—for them, and no others. So far as the *Cloud* is concerned, he forbids any but those seeking spiritual advancement to read it:

'I charge thee and I beseech thee, with as much power and virtue as the bond of charity is sufficient to suffer, . . . that thou neither read it, write it, nor speak it, nor yet suffer it to be read, written, or spoken, by any other or to any other, unless it be by such a one or to such a one as hath in thy supposing in a true will and by a whole intent purposed him to be a perfect follower of Christ.'[3]

The reason for this strict prohibition is that the author feared his teaching might be misunderstood. This fear is not groundless. The doctrine and discipline advocated by the *Cloud* are not intended for universal adoption; they can easily lead to perilous excesses and even dangerous follies. The strong injunction that the book should be read only under the guidance of some spiritual director was necessary.

The *Cloud* was first written for a young man, twenty-four years old, already a religious, who had made some progress in contemplative life; it was also intended for others of like mind and heart who might benefit by its

[1] *The Cloud of Unknowing*, &c., by Dom Justin McCann, p. xiv. References throughout this chapter, unless otherwise stated, will be to this volume.
[2] See also *Sense and Thought*, a study in mysticism, based upon the *Cloud*, by Greta Hort, M.A., Ph.D. Advanced students will enjoy this clever psychological study; but beginners may find it too technical and abstract.
[3] Prologue, p. 3.

advice and teaching. It is not surprising that the author frequently calls upon his pupil to brace up his mind and will as he faces the contents of this treatise. We ourselves shall not have gone far in reading it before we discover that since leaving Richard Rolle we have stepped into another world. The Yorkshire hermit dealt straightforwardly with the evangelical facts of the Gospel story; this writer is daringly speculative in his treatment of certain matters of the Faith, especially the Deity and the soul's approach thereto. Rolle glowed with the fire of love when he thought of his Saviour as the Friend of sinners; this writer can kindle when he thinks of our Lord, as he often does, in this way: but when he is concerned with the Christ of the Godhead, and His relations to the veiled and mysterious Absolute, his fervour has not the same sparkle. Rolle's style of writing, like his message, was personal and practical; this man's, like his thought, is at times intricate, and not a little obscure. Our anonymous author belongs to a different school from Rolle; he is an ardent admirer of Dionysius the Areopagite. To our author, the works of this unknown Syrian monk of the early sixth century were second only in value and authority to the Bible. As an act of gratitude he translated Dionysius' *Mystical Theology* into English; he also strove to simplify his master's teaching by giving it a more popular form in this work, *The Cloud of Unknowing*.

Reference was made in the first chapter to Dionysius and his twofold method of approach to God: the *affirmative* and *negative way*. It will help to a clearer understanding of the *Cloud* if we give here a little fuller consideration to the latter of these two ways. Dionysius, as we saw, had a preference for the *negative way*. His choice was determined by his Neoplatonic philosophy: a system of thought which went back through Proclus and Plotinus to Plato. It emphasized the transcendence of God: He is above and beyond every form of existence and of human perception. It is impossible to say anything about Him, except that He is the Absolute No-thing. Such teaching would seem to border on Nihilism; but we only think that if we become impatient with his negations and denials. Dionysius has, as he believes, excellent reasons for raising God to these super-heights. He held that God was so exalted in His essence and majesty as to be beyond man's apprehension; neither could He, in the fulness of His Being, be expressed in human language. Moreover, it was a basic principle with Dionysius that the Divine unity and impeccability must be preserved; hence, he had to remove God from all possible contact with matter and the creatures, because these were subject to change and decay, divisibility and imperfection. He is sure, however, that God can be reached: union between Him and the human soul is possible. Man attains this blessed state by rising above the world of space and time, by freeing himself from all creatures, and by lifting himself above all the powers and faculties of his mind and body.[1] So it is that man, as Dionysius says in his *Mystical Theology*, by a *process of unknowing*, enters 'into the Darkness where truly dwells, as the Scripture saith, that One which is beyond all things',[2] and here he is granted the soul's supreme reward: the vision of the super-essential One. Dionysius describes the process:

'I counsel that, in the earnest exercise of mystic contemplation, thou leave the senses and the activities of the intellect and all things that the senses or the intellect can perceive, and all things in this world of nothingness, or in that world of being, and that, thine understanding being laid to rest, thou strain (so far as thou mayest) towards an union with Him whom neither being nor understanding can contain. For by the unceasing and absolute renunciation of thyself and all things, thou shalt in pureness cast all things aside, and be

[1] See Dr. Inge's *Plotinus*, Vol. II, Lectures XVII–XIX. Also Baron F. von Hügel's *Mystical Element of Religion*, Vol. II, pp. 90–101.
[2] Rolt's *Dionysius*, p. 193.

released from all, and so shalt thou be led upwards to the Ray of that Divine Darkness that exceedeth all existence.'[1]

If we grasp the meaning of that passage, it will help us to master the teaching we find in the *Cloud*. This teaching, we know, will not appeal to everybody; to some it will savour much more of metaphysics than of religion, and will appear coldly austere and cloudily obscure, altogether lacking in those elements of warmth, simplicity, and attractiveness which are needed to win human affection and devotion. Perhaps this type of teaching, which has had many notable advocates, was carried to its finest logical issues in relation to mystical experience by St John of the Cross, who brought to its treatment scientific precision, psycho-analytical skill, and a saint's fervour: and to it he has given classical expression. But before we dismiss Dionysius—or those who follow him—on account of our antipathy to his method, we should remember he is trying to do one thing at least for which we ought to be thankful. He seeks to reconcile the antithesis which confronts us everywhere: in creation, human life, and the Scripture: that God is the Unknown, and yet the Well-Known; the Hidden, and yet the Revealed; the One who withholds Himself, and yet the One who gives Himself. As the Bible puts it: 'He made darkness His hiding place' (Ps. xviii. 11), and yet, 'God is light and in Him is no darkness at all' (1 John i. 5). Hence, with Dionysius, the Divine Darkness is 'most luminous', and if we enter into It our souls will be flooded with incomparable light.

Our author accepts all this. He believes that the only way to God is by a 'process of unknowing'; he actually quotes the sentence from Dionysius, 'The most godly knowing of God is that which is known by unknowing'.[2] So, like the Areopagite, he bids us leave behind the worlds of thought, of imagination, of the senses, and all their mental and material associations; by this act we come to a

---

[1] Rolt, p. 191.   [2] *Cloud*, Ch. 70.

condition of ignorance or unknowing. In that 'blind' state, by a supreme effort of the soul, we must try to touch Divine Reality. We shall then find, however, that we are confronted with a 'Cloud of Unknowing': this is between us and God. We must not turn from this in disappointment or despair, for within its dark and lustrous folds is the Goal of our endeavour: there we shall attain union with the Godhead: there discover and enjoy Divine Life, and Love, and Light; all the treasures for which our soul has sought. How shall we penetrate this 'Cloud'? By ceaseless acts of will—the will sharpened and strengthened by love. To these acts or impulses he gives suggestive and poetic names: 'a naked intent', 'blind' and 'sudden stirrings', 'a sharp dart of longing love', 'a blind stirring unto God and a secret setting upon this cloud of unknowing'. Many similar metaphorical expressions will be found throughout the book; they all really describe the soul's concentrated efforts in prayer, especially its aspirations, elevations, and uprisings. More often than not, however, these constant acts of will—these ceaseless upward thrustings of the soul in prayer—are summed up in the single word 'work': in the performance of this work, in 'beating on this dark cloud of unknowing', the soul wins through to its reward. This is how the author describes that work:

'Lift up thine heart unto God with a meek stirring of love; and mean Himself and none of His goods. And thereto look that thou loathe to think on aught but Himself, so that nought work in thy mind nor in thy will but only Himself. And do that in thee is to forget all the creatures that ever God made and the works of them, so that thy thought or thy desire be not directed or stretched to any of them, neither in general nor in special.'[1]

'But ever when thou feelest thy mind occupied with no manner of thing that is bodily or ghostly, but only with the

[1] Ch. 3.

very substance of God, as it is and may be in the proof of the work of this book: then thou art above thyself and beneath thy God.'[1]

Here is what he says of the *darkness* in which, and beyond which, God dwells, and to which we must direct our 'naked intent'; at the same time he defines the *cloud of unknowing*:

'Cease not, therefore, but travail in this work till thou list.[2] For at the first time when thou dost it, thou findest but a darkness, and as it were a *cloud of unknowing*, thou knowest not what, saving that thou feelest in thy will a naked intent unto God. This darkness and this cloud, howsoever thou dost, is betwixt thee and thy God, and hindereth thee, so that thou mayest neither see Him clearly by light of understanding in thy reason, nor feel Him in sweetness of love in thine affection. And therefore shape thee to bide in this darkness as long as thou mayest, evermore crying after Him whom thou lovest. For if ever thou shalt see Him or feel Him, as it may be here, it must always be in this cloud, and in this darkness. And if thou wilt busily travail as I bid thee, I trust in His mercy that thou shalt come thereto.'[3]

'And ween not, because I call it a darkness or a cloud, that it is any cloud congealed of the vapours that fly in the air, or any darkness such as in thine house on nights, when the candle is out. For such a darkness and such a cloud mayest thou imagine with curiosity of wit, for to bear before thine eyes in the lightest day of summer; and also contrariwise in the darkest night of winter thou mayest imagine a clear shining light. Let be such falsehoods; I mean not thus. For when I say darkness, I mean a lacking of knowing: as all things that thou knowest not, or hast forgotten, is dark to thee; for thou seest it not with thy ghostly eye. And for this reason it is called, not a cloud of the air, but a *cloud of unknowing*; which is betwixt thee and thy God.'[4]

As we have seen, our author insists that we must completely free ourselves from all creatures and created things; here he explains how this is to be done:

[1] Ch. 67.　　[2] To feel zest or desire.　　[3] Ch. 3.　　[4] Ch. 4.

'Thou thinkest, peradventure, that thou art full far from God, because this *cloud of unknowing* is betwixt thee and thy God; but surely, if it be well conceived, thou art full further from Him when thou hast no *cloud of forgetting* betwixt thee and all the creatures that ever be made. As oft as I say "all the creatures that ever be made", so oft do I mean, not only the creatures themselves, but also all the works and the conditions of the same creatures. I except not one creature, whether they be bodily creatures or ghostly; nor yet any condition or work of any creature, whether they be good or evil. But, to speak shortly, all should be hid under the *cloud of forgetting* in this case.'[1]

None the less, let us hasten to stress the fact that our author is no Neoplatonist; nor does he slavishly follow Dionysius. The veiled and mysterious Ultimate of the metaphysician does not satisfy the longing heart of this earnest seeker after the Divine. In his search for God he was wonderfully helped by the ever-present Christ; as a result, a warm spring of personal feeling mingles with the cold stream of abstract discussion, and radically changes the temperature of his experiences—and of his writings. A further consequence of this contact with Christ is that in the soul's effort to apprehend God, our author does not lay the same emphasis as Dionysius on the work of the intellect in its task of simplification and negation; rather, like other great Christian teachers—especially of the West —he stresses the efficacy of love, the purest and strongest passion of the soul. This is apparent in the following comparison between the power of thought and the power of love:

'All reasonable creatures, angel and man, have in them, each one by himself, one principal working power, the which is called a knowing power, and another principal working power, the which is called a loving power. Of the which two powers, to the first, God who is the maker of them is evermore incomprehensible; but to the second, He is, in every man

[1] Ch. 5.

diversely, all comprehensible to the full. Insomuch that one loving soul alone in itself, by virtue of love, may comprehend in itself Him who is sufficient to the full—and much more, without comparison—to fill all the souls and angels that may be. And this is the endless marvellous miracle of love.'[1]

Later on, he puts the same truth in another setting; here he describes love by one of his favourite mystical phrases, and then, on a flood of moving words, shows that love can do what nothing else can, even to the point of casting out sin:

'And therefore, if thou wilt stand and not fall, cease never in thine intent, but beat evermore on this *cloud of unknowing* that is betwixt thee and thy God with a sharp dart of longing love. And loathe to think on aught under God. And go not thence for anything that befalleth. For this only by itself is that work that destroyeth the ground and root of sin. Fast thou never so much, watch thou never so long, rise thou never so early, wear thou never so sharp;[2] yea, and if it were lawful to do—as it is not—though thou put out thine eyes, cut thy tongue out of thy mouth, stop up thy nose and thine ears never so fast, shear away thy members, and do all the pain to thy body that thou mayest or canst think: all these will help thee right nought. Yet will stirring and rising of sin be in thee.'[3]

To the question, 'How shall I think on God, and what is He?' he answers, 'I know not'; but once more, where thought cannot enter, love opens the door:

'For thou hast brought me with thy question into that same *cloud of unknowing* that I would thou wert in thyself. For all other creatures and their works—yea, and of the works of God Himself—may a man through grace have fullness of knowing, and well can he think of them; but of God Himself can no man think. And therefore I would leave all that thing that I can think, and choose to my love that thing that I cannot think. For why, He may well be loved, but not thought. By love may He be gotten and holden; but by thought never.'[4]

The former part of the above passage will warn us

___

[1] Ch. 4.   [2] a hair shirt.   [3] Ch. 12.   [4] Ch. 6.

against assuming that the writer is anti-intellectualist. Whilst he believes that the grace of contemplation is the highest gift God bestows, and that it is independent of intellectual achievement, he yet has much to say in many places in praise of learning, knowledge, and wisdom. Thus, if we ask what it is within us that presses us to seek God, he says:

'It is a sharp and clear beholding of thy natural wit, printed in thy reason within in thy soul. And where thou askest me whether it is good or evil: I say that it must always be good in its nature; for it is a beam of the likeness of God.'[1]

To a few elect souls—the choice is always with God— this grace of contemplation may be granted without long travail,[2] but the author insists that upon all other aspirants this work will make stringent demands. Moreover, if, by God's goodness, anything of reward is granted in this life, it may come at the end of what might prove an extended process of instruction and testing. This fact of prolonged discipline comes out in his teaching concerning the 'two manner of lives in Holy Church'; the active and the contemplative: active life

'is both begun and ended in this life; but not so contemplative life. For it is begun in this life, and shall last without end.'[3]

Speaking of the nature of these lives he says that each has two parts, a higher and a lower. However, the higher part of active life and the lower part of contemplative life overlap, so that we get three lives: active, mixed, and contemplative; or, they may be regarded as three stages of the one life. He sets out fully the functions of each part:

'The lower part of active life standeth in good and honest bodily works of mercy and of charity. The higher part of active and the lower part of contemplative life lieth in good ghostly meditations, and busy beholdings unto a man's own

[1] Ch. 8.   [2] Ch. 71.   [3] Ch. 8.

wretchedness with sorrow and contrition, unto the passion of Christ and of His servants with pity and compassion, and unto the wonderful gifts, kindness, and works of God in all His creatures, bodily and ghostly, with thanking and praising. But the higher part of contemplation (as it may be here) hangeth all wholly in this darkness and in this *cloud of unknowing*, with a loving stirring and a blind beholding unto the naked being of God Himself only.'[1]

The full fruition of contemplative life will be manifest and enjoyed, in the clear vision of the Beloved, in eternity. Meantime, the blessing of this work on earth is very great all round; it not only wins the favour of the inhabitants of heaven, it also has other far-reaching effects. In these days, when everybody is urged to cultivate the spirit of the good neighbour, it is worth pointing out that our author claims special value of this kind for the saintly life. So potent is its influence that besides helping our friends and society generally, it assists the departed in the intermediate state:

'For one thing I will tell thee: it is more profitable for the health of thy soul, more worthy in itself, and more pleasing to God and to all the saints and angels in heaven—yea! and more helpful to all thy friends, bodily and ghostly, quick and dead—such a blind stirring of love unto God for Himself, and such a secret setting upon this *cloud of unknowing*, and thou wert better to have it and feel it in thine affection ghostly, than to have the eyes of thy soul opened in contemplation or beholding of all the angels or saints in heaven, or in hearing of all the mirth and melody that is among them in bliss.'[2]

'All men living on earth be wonderfully helped by this work, thou knowest not how. Yea, the souls in purgatory are eased of their pains by virtue of this work.'[3]

Still speaking of the seeker's reward, he refers to one of the mystic's highest experiences: the flash of divine illumination which communicates to the soul heavenly truth

[1] Ch. 8, and see Ch. 21.   [2] Ch. 9.   [3] Ch. 3.

and radiance—though the intimacy of the revelation and the intensity of the joy are impossible to express:

'Then will He sometimes peradventure send out a beam of ghostly light, piercing this *cloud of unknowing* that is betwixt thee and Him, and show thee some of His secrets, the which man may not and cannot speak. Then shalt thou feel thine affection inflamed with the fire of His love, far more than I can tell thee, or may or will at this time. For of that work that pertaineth only to God dare I not take upon me to speak with my blabbering fleshly tongue: and, shortly to say, although I durst I would not.'[1]

In seeking these supreme blessings of the prayer-life, the soul will naturally avail itself of every form of prayer. The prayers of Holy Church will not be neglected 'in the form and in the statute that they are ordained by holy fathers before us'. The more advanced forms—vocal and mental—will also be practised. So the ardent soul will be carried forward to the highest states of contemplation and union, 'the spiritual marriage', when the soul and the Beloved are one, and prayer is vision. In any of these stages the earnest seeker will also use spontaneous prayer; for these unpremeditated cries best express the urgency and need of the soul, when it craves for a swift response of Divine Love. Single words, preferably of one syllable, are most effective. Just as, in the same way, if any one is affrighted by fire, and wishes to warn others, he does not cry out in many words, or even in a word of two syllables: he just shouts FIRE! or OUT!

'And right as this little word FIRE stirreth rather and pierceth more hastily the ears of his hearers, so doth a little word of one syllable, when it is not only spoken or thought, but secretly meant in the depth of the spirit. And rather it pierceth the ears of Almighty God than doth any long psalter unmindfully mumbled in the teeth. And therefore it is written that short prayer pierceth heaven.'[2]

[1] Ch. 26.　　　　　　　[2] Ch. 37.

THE CLOUD OF UNKNOWING'

Particularly when the soul is aflame with love, let it not attempt to restrain its rapture, but let it cry out with gladness of spirit, using tender and affectionate phrases which breathe the joyous Name. He says:

'I will not that thou desist any time, if thou be stirred to pray with thy mouth, or to burst out, for abundance of devotion in thy spirit, for to speak unto God as unto man, and say some good word as thou feelest thyself stirred: as be these, "Good Jesu! Fair Jesu! Sweet Jesu!" and all such other.'[1]

But this experienced servant of God is careful to warn his young disciple not to set too much store on these sensible delights, and not to hanker after them. If God sends them let them be enjoyed; but if He withholds them let there be no complaint. We should remember too that wicked spirits can simulate these joys in our heart:

'As a reward, God will sometimes inflame the body of a devout servant of His here in this life with full wonderful sweetness and comforts. Of the which, some be not coming from without into the body by the windows of our wits, but from within, rising and springing from abundance of ghostly gladness, and from true devotion of spirit. Such a comfort and such a sweetness shall not be held suspect. . . . But all other comforts, sounds, and gladness, and sweetness, that come from without suddenly, and thou knowest never whence, I pray thee have them suspect. For they may be both good and evil, wrought by a good angel or by an evil angel.'[2]

On the other hand, should the soul for a time have to dwell in a dry and thirsty land, where no water is, enduring torturing doubt and sorrow, let it not be anxious or afraid. In its efforts to penetrate the *cloud of unknowing*, where it would hold happy and continuous fellowship with God, it will be constantly thwarted by the consciousness of its own being: the earthly, sensual, rebellious part of its nature will drag it down. Let not the soul at such a time grow desperate; never let it entertain the wild wish

[1] Ch. 48.   [2] Ch. 48.

that it might expire. For this desolation, if rightly understood, is full of holy desire, which must ultimately prevail.

'For as oft as he would have a true knowing and feeling of his God in purity of spirit, and then feeleth that he may not —for he findeth evermore his knowing and his feeling as it were occupied and filled with a foul stinking lump of himself, the which must always be hated and despised and forsaken, if he shall be God's perfect disciple, taught by Himself in the mount of perfection—so oft he goeth nigh mad for sorrow. Insomuch, that he weepeth and waileth, striveth, curseth and denounceth himself; and (shortly to say) he thinketh that he beareth so heavy a burden of himself that he careth never what betides him, so that God were pleased. And yet in all this sorrow he desireth not to un-be: for that were devil's madness and despite unto God. But he liketh right well to be; and he giveth full heartily thanks unto God, for the worthiness and gift of his being, although he desire unceasingly for to lack the knowing and the feeling of his being.'[1]

From these quotations it will be apparent that this fourteenth-century monastic was a loyal son of the Church; yet he was by no means a slave to convention or tradition. He realized, like the sturdy men of a later age, that in the commerce between God and the soul, there must be room for freedom and spontaneity. His views on spiritual discipline and the mortification of the flesh were just as sane and progressive. He acknowledged that for some people ascetic practices might serve a useful purpose; but they should never be undertaken, least of all by a beginner, apart from an irresistible inward conviction, which itself must be confirmed by some trustworthy outward authority. For a successful prosecution of this work of the soul, we must carefully watch our condition; mental and physical fitness are as far as possible to be preserved.[2] He also begs eager souls, when they approach God, to cultivate a calm and even spirit, and not to be aggressive

---

[1] Ch. 44; and see *Privy Counsel*, Ch. 8.
[2] *Cloud*, Ch. 41.

in their demands, or violent in their methods; he puts the point smilingly:

'And abide courteously and meekly the will of our Lord, and snatch not over-hastily, as it were a greedy greyhound, though thou hunger never so sore. And, to speak playfully, I counsel that thou do what in thee is to refrain the rude and the great stirring of thy spirit, as though thou wouldst on nowise let Him know how fain thou wouldst see Him or feel Him.'[1]

The results of this inward work are seen in a glad, beautiful, and attractive life, which others beholding will wish to copy:

'Whoso hath this work, it should govern them full seemly, as well in body as in soul: and make them full favourable unto each man or woman that looked upon them. Insomuch, that the worst-favoured man or woman that liveth in this life, if they might come by grace to work in this work, their favour should suddenly and graciously be changed, so that each good man that saw them should be fain and joyful to have them in company, and full much they should think that they were pleased in spirit and helped by grace unto God in their presence.'[2]

In a searching passage he contrasts the truly changed man with men of mere pretence, and describes by what methods these hypocrites try to counterfeit the true spiritual possessions; for these imitators—who are not prepared to pay the price to get the real thing—he feels the keenest scorn: 'the devil's contemplatives',[3] he brands them. These deceits are sometimes caused by ignorance, especially amongst the young and inexperienced. Such beginners have no real understanding of what is to be aimed at, nor do they practise right methods; the results are deplorable:

'And in this manner is the madness wrought that I speak of. They read and hear well said that they should leave out-

---

[1] Ch. 46.   [2] Ch. 54.   [3] Ch. 45.

ward working with their wits, and work inwards: and because they know not which is inward working, therefore they work wrong. For they turn their bodily wits inward into their body against the course of nature; and they strain them, as though they would see inwards with their bodily eyes, and hear inwards with their ears, and so forth with all their wits, smelling, tasting, and feeling inwards. And thus they reverse them against the course of nature, and with this curiosity they travail their imagination so indiscreetly that at the last they turn their brain in their heads; and then as fast the devil hath power to feign some false light or sounds, sweet smells in their noses, wonderful tastes in their mouths, and many quaint heats and burnings in their bodily breasts or in their bowels, in their backs and in their reins and in their members.'[1]

Where the consequences are not so serious, wrong ideas or methods may still lead to objectionable and ridiculous practices. The author's famous fifty-third chapter is a mocking description of the 'wonderful gestures' of 'hypocrites and heretics' who in most outlandish ways try to impress people with their devotion and piety. Our author is merciless: they

'stare as though they were mad, and leeringly look as if they were the devil; some set their eyes in their heads as though they were sturdy sheep beaten in the head; some hang their heads on one side as if a worm were in their ears; some pipe when they should speak as if there were no spirit in their bodies; some cry and whine in their throats. . . . Some can neither sit still, stand still, nor lie still, unless they either be wagging with their feet, or else somewhat doing with their hands; some row with their arms in the time of their speaking, as though they needed to swim over a great water; some be smiling and laughing at every other word they speak, as they were giddy girls or silly jesting jugglers lacking behaviour. These unseemly and disordered gestures be very tokens of unstableness of heart and unrestfulness of mind, and especially of the lacking of the work of this book.'[2]

[1] Ch. 52.   [2] Ch. 53.

Our author's strong aversion to these quaint antics appears again in his charming *Epistle of Discretion*, where, with a gentle touch of irony, he dubs them as being 'on the ape's manner, for the ape doth as he seeth others do'.[1] In addition to these pretenders, other classes come under his lash. Like Richard Rolle, he had been pestered with busybodies who went about putting everybody else in their place—by their interference creating trouble. Without mincing words he tells these fussy ecclesiastics the source of their officiousness: 'it is the fire of hell welling up in their brains and their imagination'.[2] In an earlier chapter he writes with stinging contempt of those who are puffed up with vanity on account of their learning, and use it to secure their own advancement, 'in coveting of worldly dignities and having of riches and vain delights and flatterings of others'.[3] He is just as harsh in his treatment of heretics. In the following passage he is probably referring to the Lollards, and to their supporters, the anti-clerical nobility:

'Some there be that, for pride and curiosity of natural wit and letterly knowledge leave the common doctrine and counsel of Holy Church. And these with all their favourers lean overmuch to their own knowing. And because they were never grounded in meek blind feeling and virtuous living, therefore they merit to have a false feeling, feigned and wrought by the ghostly enemy. Insomuch that at the last they burst up and blaspheme all the saints, sacraments, statutes, and ordinances of Holy Church. Fleshly living men of the world, the which think the statutes of Holy Church over hard for them to amend their lives by, they lean to these heretics full soon and full lightly, and stalwartly maintain them, and all because they think they lead them a softer way than is ordained by Holy Church.'[4]

In *The Epistle of Privy Counsel* our author offers further direction to his disciple, probably in answer to definite

[1] *Cell of Self-Knowledge*, p. 102. [2] *Cloud*, Ch. 55. [3] Ch. 8.
[4] Ch. 56.

inquiries regarding particular points in the *Cloud*; the pupil may have found some of the instructions hard to understand and some of the practices hard to perform. Here the teacher tells him that the supreme aim of contemplative life is inward perfection, which consists in the union of the soul with God. This lifting up of the soul to God is 'the most precious offering' we can make to Him, and, when practised, is apparent in every detail of daily life:

'For in this blind beholding of thy naked being thus oned to God, as I tell thee, shalt thou do all that thou shalt do: eat and drink, sleep and wake, go and sit, speak and be still, lie and rise, stand and kneel, run and ride, travail and rest. And it shall be the chief of all thy doings, and in all thy doings, whether they be active or contemplative.'[1]

Towards the end of the Epistle, he defines, as nearly as he can, the nature of the soul's union with God, and the blessedness that flows from it. When we have become, by the glad acceptance of God's will, utterly indifferent to the presence or absence of sensible phenomena,

'In this time is thy love both chaste and perfect. In this time it is that thou both seest thy God and thy Love, and nakedly feelest Him also by ghostly oneing to His love in the sovereign point of thy spirit, as He is in Himself, but blindly as it may be here, utterly spoiled of thyself and nakedly clothed in Himself, as He is, unclothed and not lapped in any of these sensible feelings—be they never so sweet nor so holy —that may fall in this life. But in purity of spirit properly and perfectly He is perceived and felt in Himself as He is, far removed from any fantasy or false opinion that may fall in this life.'[2]

If any aspirant wishes to know whether he is called by God to this work of perfection, there are certain tests. After being cleansed in conscience according to the law of Holy Church and under the guidance of a spiritual coun-

---

[1] *Privy Counsel*, Ch. 5. [2] Ibid., Ch. 12.

sellor, there will be two sources of evidence: internal and
external. The first will be an inner compulsion of spirit:
we must do this or perish; and this in turn will be confirmed by the witness of God's Spirit to our spirit. The
second is an outward sign, because it comes to us through
our ears and eyes. In listening to conversations and readings of books, or in private meditations and readings, we
shall desire to hear and read of nothing else but this work
of the soul. If this desire persists and brings spiritual
satisfaction, it is good evidence that we are called of God
to a life of contemplation.[1]

This writer has many personal traits which recommend
him to our heart. We delight in what, for that age, was
a new note of independence:

'For once men thought it meekness to say nought of their
own heads, unless they confirmed it by Scripture and doctors'
words; and now it is turned into curiosity and display of
knowledge. For thee it needeth not, and therefore I do it
not.'[2]

His outspokenness is refreshing. Of beginners, who re-
sented God's withdrawal, for the time being, of divine
grace, he says:

'And thus ween ofttimes some young fools that God is their
enemy, when He is their full Friend.'[3]

He had to be equally plain with certain 'clerks and men
of great knowledge', who made him both mourn and
smile, especially when they said his writing was 'so hard
and so high, so curious and so quaint' that they could
scarcely understand it. He hits back by declaring that it is
because they are 'so blind in their curious knowledge of
learning and of nature' that they can't grasp the simple
meaning of a light work for plain people; so far as mental
effort is concerned, he asks no more of them than 'is

Privy Counsel, Chs. 10, 11.   [2] _Cloud_, Ch. 70.   [3] Ch. 75.

plainly proper to the lewdest cow or to the most unreasonable beast'.[1]

It is not surprising therefore that, in writing so characterized, we should find allegories and metaphors not only bold, but also striking and original:

'Take good, gracious God as He is, flat and plain as a plaster, and lay it to thy sick self as thou art.'[2]

In quite another style he writes of the difference between ghostly and natural wisdom. Natural wit is

'as the darkness of the moonshine in a mist at midwinter night from the brightness of the sunbeam in the clearest time of midsummer day.'[3]

Then he flings off neat and beautiful similes like these:

'For if this work of the soul be truly conceived, it is but a sudden stirring, and as it were unadvised, speedily springing unto God as a sparkle from the coal.'[4]

'And so furthermore at the last I would help thee to knit the ghostly knot of burning love betwixt thee and thy God, in ghostly onehead and accordance of will.'[5]

'And all this He doth because He will have thee made as pliant to His will ghostly as a Roan glove[6] to thine hand bodily.'[7]

At the conclusion of the *Cloud* he writes a golden sentence like this:

'For not what thou art, nor what thou hast been, doth God regard with His merciful eyes, but what thou wouldst be.'[8]

As we draw to a close the study of these works, definite impressions of their author will pleasantly linger in our minds. We shall cherish the conviction that we have been in the company of one who is not only a gifted exponent of the devout life, but must himself also have been a shining example of its practice. This conviction will be

---

[1] *Privy Counsel*, Ch. 1.   [2] Ibid., Ch. 2.   [3] Ibid., Ch. 5.   [4] *Cloud*, Ch. 4.
[5] Ch. 47.   [6] A leather glove, as made in Rouen.
[7] *Privy Counsel*, Ch. 12.   [8] *Cloud*, Ch. 75.

due, in no small measure, to his glowing enthusiasm for
the spiritual life, his uncompromising demands for reality
in religion, and, most of all, to the deep note of joyous
commendation which creeps into his descriptions of the
fruits of contemplative life.

Then, we are pretty sure that, while he pokes fun at
scholars whose vanity led them to air their knowledge, he
himself was a lover of the scholarly life. Many pages of
his books suggest that. We have seen with what ardour he
studied Neoplatonism, especially the Christian Neoplatonist, Dionysius the Areopagite. He had spent much
time with the Scholastics. But he also drank deeply of
more sparkling waters: at the well-springs of St. Augustine; St. Gregory and St. Bernard; Hugh and Richard St.
Victor; and his fellow-countryman, Richard Rolle. A
quotation shows that he had at least dipped his cup into
the copious waters of Aristotle.[1] While he may have
imbibed plenteously from these sources, he was no mere
conduit. He passes the teaching of these masters through
his own mind, and it comes out minted with his own
originality. His intimate knowledge of the Bible enabled
him to select from its pages the apt quotation and telling
reference which light up his writings.

We are confident he was a lovable man. We are
strengthened in this assurance by the excellent qualities
of his nature: his wit and wisdom, urbanity and frankness; his kindly interest in his pupil and in young people
generally; and his delightful eagerness to help any whom
he could possibly serve.

[1] *Privy Counsel*, Ch. 13.

CHAPTER VI

WALTER HILTON

THE *Scale of Perfection* first appeared towards the end oɪ the fourteenth century.[1] During the next one hundred years it was often copied, and it circulated in many manuscripts. In 1494 it was printed by Caxton's successor, Wynkyn de Worde; by 1533 eight editions had been published. Almost from its first issue it became a devotional classic. People of most diverse religious types have fallen beneath its spell. Thoughtful readers will soon discover the reason of this. The book answers in a most satisfying way the permanent needs of the soul. Other qualities recommend it: its contents are well arranged; its theme is clearly stated and admirably developed; its style is simple, persuasive, and quietly convincing; and throughout it is marked by lofty thought, deep insight, and sanity of judgement. Such a book could not help but make a wide appeal.

Excellent as the *Scale* is, however, we may feel a little surprise that for so long it should have taken precedence over other classics of the devout life. It has not the quaint candour and picturesque homeliness of the *Ancren Riwle*; it lacks the poetic imagery and spiritual rapture of Richard Rolle; it has not the intellectual force and sparkling humour of the *Cloud*; it does not share the strange touch of genius we find in Julian; nor for variety of interest and vividness of characterization can it compete with *The Book of Margery Kempe*. Yet in spite of these facts it is true

---

[1] On modern editions of the *Scale* see the Special Note at the end of this chapter. Extracts throughout this chapter are from Dalgairns's editioɪ.. Chapter numbers are the same as in Underhill and Noetinger.

to say that no other mystical work in our tongue has had a deeper or more abiding influence than this.

Walter Hilton was an Augustinian canon of Thurgarton, near Southwell, in Nottinghamshire. Miss Underhill, in the Introduction to her edition of the *Scale*, gives some interesting details of Thurgarton and its Priory, the ruins of which still stand, and provide some idea of its former beauty and spaciousness. She discusses, too, in a suggestive way the influence of the delightful pastoral surroundings on the mind of Hilton, as assisting to develop in him 'that gentle realism, that quiet intimacy and simplicity, which mark his teaching, with its perfect avoidance of forced contrast and exaggeration'.[1] She also gives, to complete the picture, an entertaining account of his Order, showing how active the Augustinian Canons were in religion, education, and philanthropy; yet,

'Some of his brothers in religion, judging from the records of fourteenth-century Chapters, took their vocation less earnestly; combining it with a considerable degree of worldly enjoyment. Thus in 1334 it was necessary to forbid dancing and unseemly songs. Blue capes, tight hose, and fanciful shoes were also condemned, as unsuited to the religious life; and the canons ordered to wear gaiters or jack-boots when they went abroad. In 1346 the Chapter was forced to deal with the passion for dogs—so often a difficulty in houses of religion—and prohibit the habit of feeding them in the refectory.'[2]

But to our regret, keen investigator though Miss Underhill is, she can give no fresh information about the author himself. The one definite date we can attach to Hilton is that of his death; this is given in a note on a manuscript as March 24, 1396. Beyond this useful but unilluminating fact, we know practically nothing. His is another of the fertile lives of that period which remains wrapt in obscurity. Hence with him, as with many other authors of early mystical literature, we are driven to the works

---

[1] p. x.   [2] p. xii.

themselves to learn what we can of their writer's personality.

Luckily Hilton's productions are rich in revelations of this kind. They show a man of entire devotion to our Lord, of rare humility of spirit, and with a profound admiration for the contemplative life. Along with his love of the mystical he combines a passion for the evangelical which comes out most clearly in his celebrations of the Holy Name. Though with his customary meekness, he often asserts that he himself did not practise contemplation, yet we cannot doubt he knew something of the spiritual joy of which he writes, for his words about union with Christ are quick with reality. To make him the able director of souls he was, he must have had an exceptional combination of mental and spiritual gifts: ancresses, fellow-monks, and influential men of the world, sought his guidance. His sane outlook and kindly thoughtfulness are seen in his recommendations concerning discipline: he will have no vain or foolish excesses in watchings, fastings, scourgings, or other self-inflicted austerities; the right balance of body and soul are to be kept. Altogether, his writings give the impression of a wise, kind, and gentle teacher, who found in the study, practice, and commending of contemplation his life's purpose and joy.

There has been some discussion as to whether he was a learned man. Most of his commentators think he was; Miss Underhill doubts it. She supplies but slight evidence for this opinion. She points out a curious error in the use of a Latin term,[1] but it was one of those trivial slips of which any writer might be guilty. No one can deny that for the age in which he lived he possessed a wide range of knowledge. He had been a diligent student of the great Church Fathers, particularly St. Augustine and St. Gregory, St. Bernard and St. Bonaventura; he had fruitfully studied St. Thomas Aquinas and his fellow-scholas-

[1] p. 8.

tics; but, of these recognized authorities, probably Richard of St. Victor, that bold expositor and bright exemplar of the contemplative life, had done as much as any one to stimulate his interest in mystical doctrine and experience.

In addition to these greater lights of the Church, he owed not a little to his own countrymen. There is evidence that he had read with profit the *Ancren Riwle*. For Richard Rolle he had a real affection, sometimes using his very words; but Hilton, with his more sober temperament, was a trifle afraid of the Yorkshire hermit's ecstasies, especially of the sensible phenomena—about these he gives careful warning. To the author of the *Cloud* his debt was immense; that acute thinker exercised a major influence over Hilton's mind; on many pages of the *Scale* you detect distinct traces of the earlier work. There are not a few parallels between Julian and Hilton; they may have read each other's writings.

In considering the creative forces—so far as they were human—in Hilton's spiritual development, we certainly come to the fountain-head when we name the Bible; he knew it thoroughly, accepted it implicitly, and grounded all his teaching upon it. In his quotations he gives both the Latin and English texts; this makes his extracts most valuable.

We possess three books by Hilton: the *Scale*, the *Treatise to a Devout Man*,[1] and *The Song of Angels*.[2] Other writings attributed to him are to be found in private and public libraries in this country and France. If there is anything to compare with the three already known, it is to be hoped that some enterprising publisher will in the near future rescue these manuscripts from oblivion, and give them to the world. We have seen it was thought at one time that Hilton might have written the *Cloud*. His name has also been associated with other works, most notably with that devotional masterpiece, the *Imitation of Christ*. No one

---

[1] Included in Dalgairns's edition.   [2] In *The Cell of Self-Knowledge*.

would make that claim to-day, as the authorship of Thomas à Kempis is now practically universally accepted. It is, however, a tribute to Hilton's genius that his name should have been linked to this famous book. For the time being, our author's reputation will continue to rest, as it has always done, upon the *Scale*.

The book is addressed to a 'ghostly sister in Christ Jesus'. The author says, 'Thou art bound by custom and thy rule to say thy Breviary'; further on he states, 'Right so shalt thou stand as an anchoret in that lot'; and in another place, 'Thou hast forsaken riches and the having much of this world, and art shut up in a cell'. These, and other references which could be given, make it fairly certain that he is writing for an aspirant to the contemplative life, who has passed through a nunnery, and has entered upon the solitary state in some house or cell. But it is equally clear that the writer has in mind, not only the needs of this particular person, but all who may desire to live the religious life.

The title, *The Scale*—or *Ladder of Perfection*, visualizes the soul's upward movement from the imperfect to the perfect life. Like Jacob's ladder, it is set up between earth and heaven; it leads from self to God; from the slavery of sin to the freedom of salvation; from the world of phenomena, with its multiplicity, confusion and phantasms, to the world of Reality, with its unity, order and abiding certainties. Necessarily, the climber's progress will be slow:

'But from the lowest to the highest a soul cannot suddenly start, no more than a man that would climb upon a ladder that is high, and setteth his foot on the lowest stave, can at the next step get up to the highest, but must go by degrees from one to another till he comes to the highest.'[1]

A few chapters previously, the author had given to the

---

[1] Book II, Chap. 17: the *ladder* as a figure of speech was very popular in medieval literature.

aspiring soul a most valuable hint that would help it in
its ascent to the Highest:

'And this mayest thou do the better, and the more readily,
if thou be diligent and careful to set thy heart most upon one
thing, and that is nought else but a spiritual desire after God,
how to please Him, love Him, and know Him, to see Him
and to enjoy Him by grace here in a little feeling, and in the
bliss of heaven in a full being. This desire, if thou keep it,
will tell thee what is sin, and what is not; and what thing is
good and what better; and if thou wilt but fasten thy thoughts
to the same desire, it shall teach thee all that thou needest,
and it shall procure thee all that thou wantest. Set the point
of thy thoughts more upon God whom thou desirest than upon
the sin which thou abhorrest. If thou do so, then God fighteth
for thee, and will destroy sin in thee.'[1]

The first part of the book deals with the cultivation of
the spiritual life. Though Hilton's teaching here follows
familiar lines, we will spend a little time with it, as it may
prove instructive, not merely as information, but as a
guide-book for the advancement of our own soul.

He says that in Holy Church there are two kinds of
lives by which a Christian is to be saved: active and contemplative. The active consists in the more external matters of religion: in basing character and conduct on God's
commandments, including obedience to Christ; and in
showing love and charity to those about us by deeds of
kindness and mercy. Contemplation refers more to the
internal life of religion: to the soul's ardent and deliberate
search for God, issuing in true knowledge and clear vision
of Him, which in turn will bring the soul into ever-deepening experiences of the Divine Goodness; character and
conduct, by taking on new power and fresh beauty, will
find expression in the flowering of spiritual virtues, particularly true humility, and in the exercise of perfect love and
charity amongst our fellows. Contemplative life advances

[1] Bk. I, Ch. 91.

stage by stage: first knowing—in getting a clearer sight of God by 'the opening of the eye of the soul', then feeling —especially of warmth, joy, and sweetness in Christ; last comes spiritual illumination:

'This third sort, which is as perfect as can be had in this life, consisteth both in knowing and affecting; that is, in knowing and perfect loving of God, which is when a man's soul is first reformed by perfection of virtues to the image of Jesus, and afterwards, when it pleaseth God to visit him, he is taken in from all earthly and fleshly·affections, from vain thoughts and imaginings of all bodily creatures, and, as it were, much ravished and taken up from his bodily senses, and then by the grace of the Holy Ghost is enlightened, to see by his understanding Truth itself—which is God—and spiritual things, with a soft, sweet, burning love in God, so perfectly that he becometh ravished with His love, and so the soul for the time is become one with God, and conformed to the image of the Trinity.'[1]

Because of the bodily fervours and mental delights of these experiences, he finds it necessary, like other writers on the mystical life, to say a word about the psycho-physical accompaniments. He warns his readers against visions or revelations, against all excitations of the sense, as brightness of the eye, wonderful sounding in the ear, sudden sweetness in the mouth; and especially against 'any sensible heat, as it were fire glowing and warming in the breast'. Here possibly he had in mind those who wished to be imitators of Richard Rolle. As such abnormal experiences may be wrought by both good and wicked angels, they must always be regarded with suspicion. On the other hand, if a spirit, or feeling, or revelation increases our desire,

'knitting the knots of love and devotion faster to Jesus, opening the eye of the soul into spiritual knowing more clearly, and maketh it more humble in itself, this spirit is of God'.[2]

As helps to contemplation, he recommends the usual

[1] Bk. I, Ch. 8.   [2] Bk. I, Ch. 12.

means: reading of Scripture and holy books; diligent prayer with devotion; and meditation on subjects best suited to the soul's needs. To prosecute these spiritual exercises wisely we shall need to have sincere humility— to make us feel our entire unworthiness; firm faith—in the teachings and sacraments of the Church; and a resolute will and purpose to seek after God—that we may know Him, serve Him, and love Him with all our heart. We are told that in all these works it is best to use discretion, 'for the mean is the best'.

Prayer and meditation must be constantly practised as helps. Throughout, the author insists that Prayer, in spirit, form, and purpose shall be based upon the loving study of Scripture. When the soul has been prepared by this instruction, it can use three kinds of vocal prayer: the paternoster with psalms and hymns; the ordained prayers of the Church, as matins, evensong, and hours; and spontaneous utterances inspired by the momentary experience: 'This (last) kind of prayer pleases God much, for it proceeds wholly from the heart.' It may at times be offered in the heart only, without speech, 'with great rest and quietness both of body and soul'. If in our prayer vain thoughts intrude themselves, we must just pray on and not be upset; God will accept and reward the intention. If on the other hand our heart is wondrously visited by heavenly love, we must make the most of such fervour, and keep it as long as we can—though it will make great demands upon us:

'This is a point of the passion of love, the which by great violence and mastery breaketh down and mortifieth all lusts and likings of any earthly thing, and woundeth the soul with the blessed sword of love, that it makes the body sink, not able to bear it.'[1]

He cautions beginners that even if they have these divine visitations, they should not leave vocal prayer and other

[1] Bk. I, Ch. 30.

outward exercises too soon, and give themselves wholly to meditation. Not a few enthusiastic converts to certain successful modern movements might profitably heed his wise words:

'For ofttimes in that time of rest which they take to themselves for meditation, imagining and thinking on spiritual things after their own fancies, and following their bodily feeling, having not yet received sufficient grace thereto, by indiscretion they overtravail their wits and break their bodily strength, and so fall into fancies and singular conceits, or into open errors, and hinder that grace which God hath already given them, by such vanities. The cause of all this is secret pride and overweening of themselves; for when they have felt a little grace and some sensible devotion, they esteem it so much to surpass the graces and favours He doth to others that they fall into vain-glory. Whereas if they but knew how little it were in comparison of that which God giveth, or may give, they would be ashamed to speak anything of it, unless it were in a case of great necessity.'[1]

Meditation is another help in the soul's progress. In this exercise no certain rule for every one to observe can be given, because our Lord will deal with each seeker according to his disposition, his circumstances, and his need. For example, those who have been the slaves of sin and feel sharp compunction of heart, will find their thoughts directed to His passion; while those who have not been thus defiled, but have been kept in a measure of innocency, will find their minds centred on His birth and humanity. Thus, in the practice of meditation, we shall sensibly recognize our limitations, not desiring to be treated as other than we are; and for the subject of meditation, we shall gladly receive the divine guidance, acknowledging it is the one best calculated to help us:

'Our holy Fathers heretofore taught us that we should know the measure of our gift, and therefore to work upon it, and according to it, and not take upon us, out of our head or

---

[1] Bk. I, Ch. 28; see also 'Song of Angels' in *Cell of Self-Knowledge*, pp. 68–9.

imagination, to have more in our feeling or ability than indeed we have. We may ever desire the best, but we may not ever work the best or our utmost, because we have not yet received that grace and ability.'[1]

In addition to the above helps there is, if we would further advance towards contemplation, another necessary work: a man must withdraw from external things, and enter into himself, to know his own soul and its powers. This inward sight will show the nobility and dignity of our first creation, and the wretchedness and misery we are now in as a result of our sin. This knowledge will make a man eager for deliverance, and for the restoration of his lost powers. Then it is he discovers that Jesus represents all he has lost, and he finds his need of Jesus—his soul's Lover and Saviour. What blessing there is in that Name!

'I mean not this word Jesus painted upon the wall, or written in letters on the book, or formed by lips in sound of the mouth, or framed in thy mind by imagination, for in this wise may a man void of charity find Him; but I mean Jesus Christ, that blessed Person, God and Man, Son of the Virgin Mary, whom this name betokeneth; that is all goodness, endless wisdom, love and sweetness, thy joy, thy glory, and thy everlasting bliss, thy God, thy Lord, and thy salvation.'[2]

We should live for nothing else than to desire and to know Jesus; to find Him is beyond all joy, either earthly or heavenly. We are to be like the woman of whom our Lord told in the parable—when she had lost her groat she lit a candle, and sought through the house till she found it:

'This groat is Jesus which thou hast lost, and if thou wilt find Him, light up a lanthorn, that is God's Word. . . . By this lanthorn thou shalt see where He is, and how to find Him. And if thou wilt, thou mayest together with this, light up another lanthorn, that is the reason of thy soul . . . by the

[1] *Scale*, Bk. I, Ch. 41.   [2] Bk. I, Ch. 46.

which thy soul may see all spiritual things. . . . By this lanthorn mayest thou find Jesus, that is if thou hold up this
lanthorn from underneath the bushel. That is to say, thy
reason must not be overlaid with earthly business, or vain
thoughts and earthly affections, but always upwards, above
all vain thoughts and earthly things as much as thou canst. If
thou do so, thou shalt see all the dust, all the filth and small
motes in thy house; that is to say, all fleshly loves and fears in
thy soul. . . . And thou shalt cast out of thy heart all such
sins, and sweep thy soul clean with the besom of the fear of
God, and wash it with thy tears, and so shalt thou find thy
groat, Jesus; He is thy groat, thy penny, thy heritage.'[1]

This inward sight of our soul not only reveals our lost
righteousness and beauty, but also 'the ground of sin' out
of which arise all other sins. What is it we shall find?

'Surely this; a dark and ill-favoured image of thy own soul,
which hath neither light of knowledge nor feeling of love of
God. This image, if thou behold it heedfully, is all inwrapped
and clothed with black stinking rags of sin. . . . Out of this
spring many great streams of sin, and small ones also. Just as
out of the image of Jesus, if thou be reformed in the beams of
spiritual light, will spring and ascend up towards heaven
burning desires, pure affections, wise thoughts and all comeliness of virtues. Even so out of this image spring stirrings of
pride, of envy and such other, which cast thee down from the
comeliness of a man into a beast's likeness.'[2]

The author gives a swift glance beneath the surface of
this image when he pithily defines it as 'a false and inordinate love of ourselves'. This is the fountain-head of all
our sinning, for from it flow pride, envy, anger, sloth,
covetousness, gluttony, and lechery: the seven deadly sins.
With these he deals very much in the same way as those
writers whose treatment we have already considered. He
says, too, that this image has five windows: 'these are the
five senses by which the soul goeth out of herself, and
fetcheth her delight, and seeketh her feeding in earthly

[1] Bk. I, Ch. 48.   [2] Bk. I, Ch. 52.

things, contrary to the nobility of her own nature'. His account of the dangers and misuses of the senses also resembles that of his predecessors.

It will be apparent that up to this point Hilton has followed, with a preferential stress of certain facts, the traditional line of exposition in the presentation of his subject. For the idea just introduced, that the divine image in man is mutilated by sin is, as every student knows, a favourite one with mystical writers of every age. Perhaps Hilton, in comparison with other teachers, gives it a more central place in the *Scale*, just as he subjects it to a more searching analysis; but this is because he is going to deal more thoroughly with the opposite process—the regeneration of the image: the entire reconstruction of personality, 'the issue of a new edition of our ego'.[1] Here we come upon the really distinctive part of his teaching: it is in the selection and use of original terms in describing the soul's restoration to its former glory.

This image of God, 'which in its first shaping was wonderful fair and bright, full of burning love and ghostly light',[2] was lost through the sin of Adam; hence it could not be restored by man, but by God alone. This is the work of the Lord Jesus Christ, who is both God and Man: His precious death is the ground of all reforming of man's soul, as it is also the means by which the soul is saved from hell and brought to heaven. The process of this reforming, we are told, has two stages: one is in part, and had in this life; the other is in fulness, had in a measure in this life, but in its completeness known only in the larger life to come. The reforming in part can and must be felt here and now, or the soul will never be saved:

'But this reforming is on two manners: one is in *Faith* only, another is in *Faith* and in *Feeling*. The first sufficeth to salvation, the second is worthy to have passing great reward in the bliss of heaven. The first may be had easily and in a short

---

[1] Noetinger, p. xxvi.   [2] *Scale*, Bk. II, Ch. 1.

time, the second not so, but through length of time and much spiritual pains. The first may be had, and yet the man may have together with it the stirrings and feelings of the image of sin: but if he do not voluntarily assent thereto, he may be and remain reformed in *Faith* to the likeness of God.

'But the second putteth out the liking in, and delight felt in sensual motions and worldly desires, and suffereth no such spots to abide in this image. The first is only of beginning and profiting souls, and of active men. The second is of perfect souls, and of contemplative men. For by the first reforming the image of sin is not destroyed, but it is left, as it were, all whole in feeling. But the second destroyeth the old feelings of this image of sin, and bringeth into the soul new gracious feelings, through the workings of the Holy Ghost. The first is good, the second is better, but the third, that is in the bliss of heaven, is best of all.'[1]

The reforming of Faith is accomplished by divine grace working through the appointed channels: especially the ordained sacraments of baptism and penance. These are provided to deal with original and actual sin; when sincerely believed in and faithfully practised, they prove efficacious. But the soul must believe. The act of faith is the vital factor. Hilton continually asserts that this is true of all the divine ordinances of the Church. The mere mechanics and materials of the sacraments can accomplish nothing; the spiritual attitude of the believer determines the working of grace. This repeated emphasis upon the necessity of faith distinguishes our author from some teachers of a later age, whose belief and advocacy were not a little tainted with superstition.

The reforming of Faith is not difficult to get; it is common to all members of the Church, even though they are not conscious of possessing it, and it is the promise of their salvation. But the reforming of *Feeling* is much more radical, and can only be secured by high aspiration, sustained effort, and earnest discipline:

[1] Bk. II, Ch. 5.

'But reforming in *Feeling* is only in those souls that are coming to the state of perfection, and that cannot be attained unto suddenly, but after great plenty of grace, and much and long spiritual exercising, and thereby shall a man attain thereto, and that will be after that he is first healed of his spiritual sickness, and after that all bitter passions and fleshly lusts and other old feelings are burnt out of the heart by the fire of desire: and new gracious feelings are brought in with burning love and spiritual light. Then doth the soul draw near to perfection, and to reforming in feeling.'[1]

He says, using the psychological terms of his day, that reforming of Feeling is a thorough renovation of the soul and all its faculties: 'memory, understanding, and will': terms intended to cover our intellectual, emotional, and volitional functions. Still more particularly, he says of 'reason', which is not so much a faculty of the soul, as the soul itself in its highest form of activity, when directed to God and heavenly things:

'Your reason, which is properly the image of God, through grace of the Holy Ghost, shall be clothed in a new light of truth, holiness, and righteousness, and then it is reformed in feeling. For when the soul hath perfect knowledge of God, then it is reformed.'[2]

That emphasis upon knowledge is one of the constant notes of the great mystics.

The reward of this reformation is the progressive apprehension of the Divine Being, and of the glorious qualities that spring from His eternal Nature:

'He openeth the inner eye of the soul, when He enlighteneth her reason through the touching and shining of His blessed light for to see Him and know Him, not all fully at once, but by little and little, by divers times, as the soul is able to bear it. He seeth Him not what He is, for that can no creature do in heaven nor in earth. Nor seeth he Him as He is, for that sight is only in the bliss of heaven. But he seeth Him that He

[1] Bk. II, Ch. 17.   [2] Bk. II, Ch. 31.

is an unchangeable being, a supreme power, a sovereign truth, supreme goodness, a blessed life, an endless bliss.'[1]

It will now be quite clear what Hilton means by his double reformation. In the soul's progress towards perfection, he divides the journey into two parts, instead of the usual three. His reformation of Faith corresponds to purgation. A soul is called from the love of the world, and after that is 'righted, tried, mortified, and purified'. Not every believer advances far along this first stage, and of those who do, not many move beyond it; they remain nominal Christians—nothing more. Yet some of these in active life, by their nobler character and their fuller service to God and man, certainly show the fruits of a disciplined life: they approach to contemplation.

Reformation of Feeling embraces the other two stages, the illuminative and the unitive. The eager soul leaves behind the uncertainties, the privations, and the sense of frustration belonging to the purgative way; more and more the heavenly light shines upon its pathway, bringing revelations, in most unexpected places, of new joys, new beauties, and new contacts; more and more there is a dawning consciousness of the ever-present Divine Companion; till at last, partly in this life and fully in the life to come, knowledge and feeling are fulfilled in vision. The soul, being restored to the divine likeness, has achieved its highest destiny: it is one with Him who all along was alike its Desire and its Desired:

'And verily that is the chiefest thing that Jesus loveth in a soul, that it may be made spiritual and divine in sight and in love, like to Him in grace, as He is by nature: for that shall be the end of all lovers.'[2]

One of the best known parts of Hilton's book is the long section where, under the analogy of a pilgrim's journey to Jerusalem, he describes all this—the soul's progress to contemplation, and its final reward. For, as he says, in

----

[1] Bk. II, Ch. 32.　　　　　　　　[2] Bk. II, Ch. 42.

his allegorical style, Jerusalem means *a sight of peace*, and betokens contemplation in perfect love of God.[1] In passing, it is interesting to point out that time and again these pages will remind the reader of Bunyan's immortal allegory, *The Pilgrim's Progress*: the earlier work might have been a draft of the later. The beginning of the journey is reforming in Faith, which is grounded on the teaching and laws of Holy Church. To face the journey, the pilgrim must go armed with the virtues of the Christian life, pre-eminently humility and love—twin weapons of the soul's armoury which never fail in the hour of need. To keep fit, the wayfarer will practise bodily and spiritual exercises best suited to his disposition and state. Lurking enemies—temptations and trials—are graphically described, and remedies against them recommended. Above everything else, the soul must keep alive its desire for Jesus:

'He is all, and He doth all, if thou couldst see Him. Thou dost nothing but sufferest Him to work in thy soul, and assentest to Him with great gladness of heart, that He will vouchsafe to do so in thee. Thou art nothing else but a reasonable instrument by which and in which He worketh: and therefore when thou feelest thy thoughts, through the touching of grace, taken up with the desire of Jesus, with a mighty devout will for to please Him and love Him, then think that thou hast Jesus, for He it is that thou desirest. Behold Him well, for He goeth before thee, not in bodily shape, but insensibly, by secret presence of His power. Therefore see Him spiritually if thou canst, and fasten all thy thoughts and affections to Him, and follow Him wheresoever He goeth, for He will lead thee on the right way to Jerusalem.'[2]

Hilton shows how this desire brings the soul into that experience which the mystics vividly describe in the familiar phrase, 'the dark night of the soul'. Here we have some of his most forceful and persuasive writing. He

[1] Bk. II, Ch. 21.   [2] Bk. II, Ch. 24.

starts with a text from Isaiah, 'My soul hath desired Thee in the night'. The night referred to, says the author, is not merely the space between two days, but it is also a spiritual night. For there are two days or two lights: the first a false light, is the love of this world; the second, a true light, is the perfect love of Jesus felt through grace in a man's soul:

'The everlasting love of Jesus is a true day and a blessed light. . . . And now, what man perceiveth and seeth the love of this world to be false and failing, and therefore will forsake it and seek the love of Jesus, yet may he not for all that presently feel the love of Him, but he must abide awhile in the night, for he cannot suddenly come from that one light to the other, that is from the love of the world to the perfect love of God. This night is nought else but a forbearing and a withdrawing of the thought and of the soul from earthly things by great desire and yearning for to love and see and feel Jesus and spiritual things. . . . And if he come to this pass then it is night with him, for then he is in darkness. But this is a good night and a light darkness, for it is a stopping out of the false love of the world, and it is an approaching of the true day. And verily the darker this night is the nearer is the true day of the love of Jesus.'[1]

If we would know whether we are in this 'secure', 'restful', and 'profitable' darkness, there is a sure test: can the soul reject every other appeal—of the bodily senses, worldly thoughts, vain imaginations, and desire Jesus only? If so, the darkness is safe, and will soon be past. For this desire of the love of Jesus felt in the darkness slays all sin, all fleshly affections, and all unclean thoughts; and so the soul, hastening to draw near to Jerusalem, sees preliminary gleams of the awaiting glory:

'Thou art not there yet, but by some small sudden lightnings that glide out of the small caves of that city, shalt thou be able to see it afar off ere thou come to it, for know thou well,

[1] Bk. II, Ch. 24.

though that thy soul be in this restful darkness without the trouble of worldly vanities, it is not yet clothed all in light, nor turned all into the fire of love. But it perceiveth full well that there is somewhat above itself that it knoweth not, nor hath not yet, but would have it, and burningly yearneth after it, and that is nought else but the sight of Jerusalem.'[1]

In a word, if a man would come to the perfect love of God, he must die to the world; and so he finds the entrance to abundant life:

'This dying to the world is this darkness, and it is the gate of Contemplation, and to reforming in feeling, and none other than this. There may be many sundry ways, and several works letting and leading sundry souls to Contemplation: for according to divers disposings of men, and after divers states as are religious and seculars, according as they are in, are there divers exercises in working. Nevertheless there is but one gate: for whatsoever exercise a soul useth, unless thereby he come to this knowing, and to a humble feeling of himself, and that is, that he be mortified and dead to the world, as to the love of it, and that he may feel himself sometime in this restful darkness, by the which he may be hid from the vanities of the world, as to the love of them, and that he may feel himself what he is indeed, he is not yet come to the reforming in feeling, nor hath he Contemplation fully.'

'This is, then, a good darkness, and a rich nought, that bringeth a soul to so much spiritual ease, and so quiet softness.'[2]

Finally, there is the reward, the blessed inward vision:

'And thus is the soul made humble, as I understand, by the working of the Holy Ghost, that is, the gift of love: for He openeth the eye of the soul to see and to love Jesus, and He keepeth the soul in that sight restfully and securely: and He slayeth all the stirrings of pride wonderfully and privily and softly, and the soul knoweth not how.'[3]

From this section on 'the dark night' two facts emerge: Hilton's indebtedness to *The Cloud of Unknowing*; and his

[1] Bk. II, Ch. 25.   [2] Bk. II, Ch. 27.   [3] Bk. II, Ch. 37.

qualified acceptance of the opinions of Dionysius. These two facts in turn reveal a third: Hilton's independence of mind. We saw that while the author of the *Cloud* was a great admirer of Dionysius, he would by no means follow him into those realms of thick darkness where Dionysius desired to lead the aspirant to the contemplative life; the writer of the *Cloud* would advance along the *negative way* only as far as was necessary for a true purgation of the soul. Hilton showed even greater caution; he would not advance as far as his predecessor. Hilton's treatment of the 'darkness' contains but a moderate element of negation, and not a hint of the stark and empty nothingness of the Areopagite.

On this same subject of 'the dark night' Hilton's name has been linked with that of St. John of the Cross. Dom Knowles has said, 'It is impossible to resist the conclusion that this state is the same as that described by St. John under the name of the Dark Night of the Senses'.[1] Even more positively Noetinger claims, '. . . the teaching of the two writers is identical'.[2] This is hard to accept. St. John conducts the soul through a threefold night—of the senses; of the understanding and reason; and of memory and will—which in the end brings the soul into a state of oblivion. How different is the soul's pilgrimage to Jerusalem, where gleams of golden sunlight constantly break on the pathway. That first part of the Spaniard's journey is like passing through a wilderness in winter time; by comparison, the Englishman's resembles a walk through one of our lovely Northern dales in spring.

A word may be added about our author's two smaller works. The *Treatise to a Devout Man* was produced for a friend who had sought Hilton's guidance. He was a man of honourable standing in the world, with wealth, large possessions, and many servants. The *Treatise* is a tract containing the application of the teaching of the *Scale* to

---

[1] *The English Mystics*, p. 120.   [2] Noetinger, p. xxxvii.

a particular case. There is one difference. Hilton recommends his inquirer to live a *mixed* life; this is a blend of *active* and *contemplative* lives: the external works of love and mercy of the one, and the internal joys and comforts of the other. In a striking figure, which conveys the gist of the tract's teaching, Hilton warns this friend against neglecting his family responsibilities and social duties for the pursuit of spiritual exercises; this will displease God:

'In so doing thou art careful to do honour and worship to His head and to His face, and to deck and adorn them fairly and curiously, but thou neglectest and leavest His body, with the feet, ragged and rent, and takest no care nor heed of them.'[1]

The Song of Angels is addressed to a 'Dear brother in Christ'—probably a fellow-monk. It is a charming little work, with distinct traces of Dionysian doctrine, and of Richard Rolle's *Fire of Love*. After describing the joys of *onehead* with God, he says:

'Also, our Lord comforteth a soul by angel's song. What that song is, it may not be described by no bodily likeness, for it is ghostly, and above all manner of imagination and reason. It may be felt and perceived in a soul, but it may not be shewed. Nevertheless, I shall speak thereof to thee as me thinketh. When a soul is purified by the love of God, then is the eye of the soul opened to behold ghostly things, as virtues and angels and holy souls, and heavenly things. Then is the soul able because of cleanness to feel the touching, the speaking of good angels. This touching and speaking, it is ghostly and not bodily. . . . Not that this song of angels is the sovereign joy of the soul. . . . For the sovereign and essential joy is in the love of God by Himself and for Himself.'[2]

This high and pure love is the fruit of prolonged discipline; hence the concluding words of this choice letter are a solemn warning to all would-be mystics:

'Lo, I have told thee in this matter a little as me thinketh;

[1] *Treatise*, Ch. VI.   [2] *Cell of Self-Knowledge*, pp. 66–7,

not affirming that this sufficeth, nor that this is the soothfast-
ness in this matter. But if thou think it otherwise, or else any
other man savour by grace the contrary hereto, I leave this
saying, and give stead to him, *It sufficeth to me for to live in truth
principally, and not in feeling.*'[1]

As we read and re-read Hilton's works, certain qualities
of his mind stand out with growing sharpness, and increas-
ingly commend him to our heart: qualities that seldom
fail to win the admiration of our people.

For instance, there is his devotion to the Bible. Here
we stress the point that Hilton was not only a faithful
student of the Word, but also a true lover. The Scriptures
fed the springs of his soul. His sweetest praises flow as he
tells of his joy in meditating upon the holy pages. He
wants everybody to share this grace—for it may be found
'as well in laymen as in learned'. Though some of his
sharpest arrows were shot at the Lollards, he must have
felt a real sympathy with Wycliffe in his courageous efforts
to put God's Word into the hands of everybody, especially of the masses in the towns and the toilers on the
land.

Again, Hilton never tires of pleading for the practice
of humility and charity; as twin virtues they are funda-
mental to character and conduct, to everything worthy
in the Christian life; as trusty weapons they will scatter
our foes on the pilgrim-way; and as glad offerings of our
soul they will open doors into the Divine Presence. As
regards humility, no Christian teacher ever strove more
earnestly to implement his own words; on many a page
you find delightful and naïve expressions like this:

'And truly this is my own case, who feel myself so wretched,
frail, and fleshly, and so far from the true feeling of that which
I speak of, that in a manner I do nothing but cry God mercy,
and desire after it as well as I can, with a hope that our Lord
will bring me thereto in heaven.'[2]

---

[1] *Cell of Self-Knowledge*, pp. 72–3,   [2] *Scale*, Bk. I, Ch. 16.

His charity was as broad as his humility was deep. Considering the age in which he lived his tolerance was remarkable. He seems so ready to make allowances where necessary, and will at times provide excuses for the recalcitrant. This excellent spirit breaks down now and again, as when he refers to Jews and Saracens, and even to an unbaptized infant—'an image of the fiend and a brand of hell'.[1] But he is at his severest when he denounces 'heretics and hypocrites': it is the Lollards he has in mind; with these, to our regret, he is much too extreme. With all others he is prepared to observe his own principle:

'Many men do deeds of charity, and have no charity. To reprove a sinner for his sin to his amendment, in a convenient time, is a deed of charity; but to hate the sinner instead of the sin, is against charity.'[2]

Then, there is his emphasis upon character. Though we refer to this briefly, it must not be regarded lightly. There is a sense in which it could be said that everything Hilton wrote was intended to press home the necessity for *reality* in religion. He was a devoted son of the Church; he loved the servants, services, and ordinances of the Church; he also realized the value of ascetical practices. But in all these he never mistook the means for the end; and that one end was Christian character—the production of Christ-like men. With Hilton, personality was bigger than system, creed, or ritual. For this we admire him.

We must point out, too, that there are some notable omissions in Hilton. He has little to say about the sacrament of mass, about priestly authority, or about the grace of celibacy. These are significant silences: they hint at the struggles of the next age, and at the emancipations of the age following that.

In conclusion, we ought to note that Hilton gained

[1] Bk. II, Ch. 6.   [1] Bk. I, Ch. 68.

remarkable facility in the use of the vernacular; he wrought it into a medium which admirably expresses his clear, chaste, and methodical mind. Such a placid and sober style does not lend itself to the epigrammatic; but at times, by the turn of a phrase, the choice of a fitting word, and the use of an apt metaphor, he does achieve some striking results. Here are one or two examples:

When the soul, living the devout life, wins its reward, 'reason is turned into light and will into love'.[1]

We should cultivate a clean heart, 'for what is a man but his thoughts and his loves'.[2]

Each one will avoid pride and vanity by remembering 'how thou art as full of sin as a hide or skin is full of flesh'.[3]

A burning heart, filled with devotion, is secure from sensual taint: 'There dare no flesh-fly rest upon the pot's brink boiling on the fire.'[4]

On studying Scripture: 'But verily he must have white teeth, and sharp, and well-picked, that can bite of this spiritual bread.'[5]

Men who seek worldly honours, goods, and riches are not wise: 'They are like to children that run after butterflies, and, because they look not to their feet, they sometimes easily fall down and break their legs.'[6]

Let a man be meek and patient, 'till he may, by custom and using of his mind, feel the fire of love in his affection, and the light of knowing in his reason'.[7]

But when our author has said all he can, he still has to confess:

'How that Presence is felt may better be known by experience than by any writing: for it is the life and the love, the might and the light, the joy and the rest of a chosen soul. And,

[1] Bk. I, Ch. 14. [2] Bk. I, Ch. 88. [3] Bk. I, Ch. 89.
[4] Bk. II, Ch. 42. [5] Bk. II, Ch. 43. [6] *Treatise*, Ch. 14.
[7] *Song*, p. 72.

therefore, he that hath once truly felt it cannot forbear it without pain, neither can he choose but desire it, it is so good in itself and so comfortable.'[1]

NOTE ON MODERN EDITIONS OF THE 'SCALE'

I debated long with myself as to which of three modern editions of the *Scale* I should use for quotation in the foregoing section.

Father Dalgairns's edition, first published in 1870, is a modernized text based upon a version issued by Serenus de Cressy in 1659, on the title-page of which Cressy claims that 'by the changing of some antiquated words it (i.e. the *Scale*) is rendered more intelligible'. A comparison of this with the two versions mentioned below will show that Cressy's changes were numerous, applying to words, phrases, and sentences: and, occasionally, to the insertion of brief explanatory clauses. This treatment admittedly had the effect of making the original 'more intelligible': but it is as well to let readers know that the text has undergone some free revision. Because its English—clear, smooth, and crisp—is so pleasant to read, this version has remained a favourite with many.

Miss Underhill's edition, dated 1923, is the outcome of first-hand study of the manuscripts. She regrets that in the 1659 version 'antiquated words'—including many of Hilton's most characteristic expressions—were replaced by seventeenth-century paraphrases or conventional equivalents. She has therefore restored as fully as possible the original text: and, while she has modernized the spelling, she has changed only entirely obsolete words into their current synonyms. Hence she claims that in her book the reader may count on coming nearer to Hilton's words and spirit, than has been possible since the black letter edition of Wynkyn de Worde. Miss Underhill has done her work most thoroughly, and has provided an edition indispensable to students and scholars.

Still another edition was published in 1927: its title-page reads, 'Modernized from the first printed edition of Wynkyn de Worde, London, 1494, by an Oblate of Solesmes'. It con-

[1] *Scale*, Bk. II, Ch. 41.

tains an informing and discriminating Introduction translated from the French of Dom M. Noetinger. As only a minimum of alteration has been made in the text, it retains a considerable amount of the Middle English of the original.

For the help of readers unfamiliar with medieval literature, it was necessary to include in each of these two later editions a rather large glossary. For many reasons I would like to have quoted from either of these restored texts—perhaps preferably from Miss Underhill's, for hers is undoubtedly the best available—but had I done so, I should have been bound either to supply a glossary or to give the equivalent words as footnotes. As I thought either course would unnecessarily interfere with the convenience of the general reader, I decided, not without reluctance, to use Dalgairns's edition. May I at once add that all lovers of the *Scale* will desire to possess both of these praiseworthy versions.

CHAPTER VII

THE LADY JULIAN

WITH the Lady Julian we are nearing the end of that short but select succession of mystics who in the fourteenth century illuminated the grey skies of this country with rays of gladsome Light. Historical comparisons are seldom fair, and often absurd; but when we see the sparkle and taste the flavour of the Lady Julian's vintage we are tempted to affirm that the best wine has been kept until last. Not a few would go further; some of the Saint's admirers are prepared to assert that in all the shining ranks of the mystics, in this and other lands, none can dim the brightness of this ancress of Norwich. Those who have fallen beneath the spell of this gracious lady, and whose interior life has been quickened by the power and beauty of her *Revelations*, will readily pardon this flicker of insular pride.

Julian introduces herself to us as 'a simple creature, unlettered', and she frequently describes herself as a 'fool' and a 'wretch', and as being 'feeble' and 'frail'; but we shall not be misled by these terms—the sincere expression of maidenly modesty. As we read her work notable qualities soon begin to obtrude themselves, and to lay an ever-tightening grip upon our admiration. She had a powerful mind which enabled her to thread her way through the labyrinths of current metaphysical thought and speculation. Her force of will gave her heroic fortitude, so that in the midst of her sufferings which brought her to the point of death she was able to laugh heartily. Her spiritual genius carried her to the highest summits of contemplative life and vision. In addition she had a rare gift of literary expression which has made her book a devotional treasure. But when we have thus described her richly-dowered nature, we feel we have not yet presented her essential personality: this can only be glimpsed in her radiant disposition, her grace and charm of manner, and her pure and loving heart wholly centred upon God.

Her book has come down to us in two forms. A shorter version, called the Amherst manuscript, has been carefully prepared for publication by the Rev. Dundas Harford, M.A., under the title, *The Shewings of Lady Julian*. He calls this the first edition, because he thinks it was written soon after the revelations ceased. There is a vigour, simplicity, and freshness about this briefer work which seems to warrant this assumption; a faint line of historical evidence supports the theory. A longer version has had some able editors in Serenus de Cressy, Father Tyrrell, Miss Grace Warrack, and Dom Roger Hudleston. Miss Warrack's edition, *Revelations of Divine Love*, based on the seventeenth-century Sloane manuscript, has enjoyed a wide circulation.[1] In the fifty-first chapter of this version the Saint says that when the revelations ended she gave the following years of her life to thought, prayer, and meditation upon them, that she might explore their hidden meaning, and elucidate their 'misty' teaching.[2] By ever-deepening fellowship with Christ she sought keener insight and clearer knowledge. At the end of twenty years she gave to her 'even-Christians' the priceless fruits of her disciplined inquiry. The result is one of the most valuable documents of ascetical experience in the whole range of mystical literature. Both versions of the book

[1] The quotations in this chapter are from this edition. Dom R. Hudleston's is a good edition, but it contains a larger sprinkling of archaic words.
[2] 'It is not the state of ecstasy alone which constitutes the certain revelation of God, but the intellectual interpretation which the mystic, restored to himself, makes of what he has experienced. Without the function of the intelligence as judge, the ecstasy would have no discernible significance.' Dr. Antonio Aliotta, in *Science, Reality, and Religion*, p. 175.

should be studied together. The earlier sketch contains words and phrases, additional passages and references—some of these last of a most interesting kind—not to be found in the later form.

The revelations took place in a house or cell built on to the little Church of St. Julian in Norwich, which, with its dark round Norman tower, is still in use, and beside which the foundations of the ruined anchorage can be traced. The only independent historical reference to the Lady Julian is in connexion with this retreat. Blomefield, in his *History of Norfolk* says, 'In 1393 Lady Julian, the ankeress here was a strict recluse, and had two servants to attend her in her old age. This woman was in these days esteemed one of great holiness'.[1] It may be that before Julian entered the anchorage she was trained and consecrated as a Benedictine nun at the adjoining Convent of Carrow. For any other information about Julian we are dependent upon her book. There we search in vain for any particulars about her parentage,[2] home, friends; or about her early interests, education, and introduction to religion: concerning these and similar matters the Saint is silent. But to compensate for these omissions, she supplies most careful descriptions of her condition—physical, mental, and spiritual—on the occasions of her visions, and she gives some most useful dates and exact times. Best of all, she entirely withdraws the veil from her inner life, and lets us see the secrets of her soul. Hence we have, for our instruction and comfort, this fascinating account of God's dealings with one of His choicest servants.

'This Revelation of Love', as Julian repeatedly describes it, came in answer to prayer. She had long desired three gifts of God: the first, a mind of Christ's Passion; the second, a bodily sickness in youth, at thirty years of age; the third, to have three wounds—the wound of contrition

---

[1] From Miss Warrack's 'Introduction', p. xvii.
[2] See note 2 on p. 134.

or kind[1] compassion, and steadfast longing towards God. The first two were asked with a condition—if they were according to God's will; the third was absolute. The first two desires passed out of her mind; the third dwelt with her continually. From this we perceive there was long and disciplined preparation on the Saint's part for the wonderful visitations she was about to enjoy.

The visions began on the 8th of May 1373, when Julian was thirty and a half years old. As a copyist reports that she was still alive in 1413, she must have reached a ripe age. She gives a vivid and detailed account of her state when the experiences started. For three days and nights she lay in serious bodily sickness. On the fourth night she took the last rites of Holy Church because she thought she could not live till day. She lingered two more days and nights. On the third night she and those with her were sure the end had come. She confesses frankly that, being yet in youth, she felt it a great sorrow to die; not because she was afraid to die, nor because she craved for life itself, but because she wanted to love God better and serve Him longer. Thus she endured till day; by that time her body was dead from the middle downwards.

'My curate was sent for to be at mine ending, and by that time when he came I had set my eyes, and could not speak. He set the Cross before my face and said: "I have brought thee the Image of thy Maker and Saviour; look thereupon and comfort thee therewith". After this my sight began to fail, and it was all dark about me in the chamber, as if it had been night, save in the Image of the Cross whereon I beheld a common light. All that was away from the Cross was of horror to me, as if it had been greatly occupied by the fiends. After this the upper part of my body began to die, so far forth that scarcely I had any feeling—with shortness of breath. And then I weened in sooth to have passed.'[2]

[1] i.e. natural.
[2] Ch. III. The Amherst MS. mentions that 'a child' came with the curate, and that Julian's mother was also present.

Quite unexpectedly there came a change: her pain completely left her, and she felt as well as she had ever done. She put this down to the working of God. Then it occurred to her to ask for the second wound she had desired: that her body might be fulfilled with the mind and feeling of Christ's blessed Passion. She says that in asking for this—and it is an important admission in face of what was about to happen—she did not wish for bodily sight and showing of God, but only for compassion such as a sympathetic soul might have for our Lord. Then the visions began:

'In this moment suddenly I saw the red blood trickle down from under the Garland hot and freshly and right plenteously, as it were in the time of His Passion when the Garland of thorns was pressed on His blessed head.'

'The great drops of blood fell down from under the Garland like pellots: the plenteousness is like to drops of water that fall off the eaves after a great shower of rain: and for roundness, they were like to the scale of herring, in the spreading on the forehead. This Shewing was quick and life-like, and horrifying and dreadful, sweet and lovely.'[1]

Fifteen Shewings succeeded one another; they started in the early morning at four, and continued until nine.[2] The Sixteenth Revelation, which was to be the completion and conclusion of all, took place the following night. Before she enjoyed this Julian suffered a serious relapse; her bodily sickness returned with all its former violence, and the spiritual comfort of the revelations fled. In this condition she was ready to believe that the visions were the ravings of delirium. But when she spoke of them to a religious person who visited her, and she observed that he listened earnestly and with great reverence, she was much ashamed of her doubt and failure. In a characteristic outburst of self-depreciation she exclaims, 'Here may you see

[1] Chs. IV and VII.   [2] Ch. LXV.

what I am of myself'. So she lay till night, trusting in God's mercy; but when she fell asleep she had a frightful nightmare:

'Methought the Fiend set him on my throat, putting forth a visage full near my face, like a young man's, and it was long and wondrous lean. He would have strangled me, but he might not. This horrible Shewing was made whilst I was sleeping, and so was none other.'[1]

It is reassuring to note how precise Julian is to stress the difference between the dream visitation and the divine spiritual illuminations. The last of her visions came that night. She gratefully describes it as a delectable Sight and Shewing, in which the good Lord assured her that He was the Author of all the previous Shewings:

'Wit it now well that it was no raving that thou sawest to-day: but take it and believe it, and keep thee therein, and comfort thee therewith, and trust thou thereto; and thou shalt not be overcome.'[2]

After this she was conscious of a deep and true peace— but not for long. The Fiend made one more effort to shake her trust and allegiance: 'He occupied me all that night, and on the morn till it was about prime day.' She successfully resisted his assaults, and adds with lofty disdain, 'I scorned him'. So far as we know this concluded these remarkable experiences, and the recluse gave herself, in the silence and solitude of the little cell, to the prayerful investigation of their contents.

Julian gives a clear statement as to the manner of the revelations:

'All this was shewed by three ways; that is to say, by bodily sight, and by word formed in my understanding, and by spiritual sight. But the spiritual sight I cannot nor may not shew it as openly nor as fully as I would.'[3]

We take this to mean that she seemed to see objects

---

[1] Ch. LXVI.   [2] Ch. LXVIII.   [3] Ch. IX.

with the bodily eye: corporeal visions. She seemed to hear
messages spoken in her mind: imaginative auditions or
locutions. She had the conviction that Truth was being
revealed to her soul: spiritual intuitions or intellectual
visions. This account corresponds to the traditional classi-
fication of revelations: corporeal, imaginative, and intellectual.[1] Julian makes no distinction in the value of these
different modes of communication: each was a medium
of Divine approach. But we are bound to remind ourselves that experts of the soul constantly utter warnings
against placing too much credence on corporeal visions
and imaginative locutions. On the other hand, they
exhort believers to seek increasing fellowship with Christ,
for in that effort comes a sharpening and refining of
spiritual perceptions; and in the resulting union, illumination of mind. It is because of her 'ghostly sight' that
Julian is such a safe and profitable guide to contemplative
life. Her spiritual faculties, by constant use, had become
so sensitive that she was susceptible to Divine Love in a
way that we cannot conceive. She herself is so over-
whelmed with the reality and marvel of these ineffable
experiences that she cannot tell us 'as openly or as fully'
as she would the wealth of her apprehensions. None the
less we thank God that we have been permitted to share
as many of the riches as she has been able to make known.

On this point of the nature of the revelations, Julian
makes another important statement. It has to do with the
growth of her knowledge of the hidden truths contained in
the original Shewings. She first admits that 'I saw and
understood that every Shewing is full of secret things left
hid'. Then she describes how, over a period of twenty
years, she 'had teaching inwardly', and enlarging illumination came in three stages:

'The first is the *beginning* of teaching that I saw therein, in

[1] For full treatment of the three kinds of experience, see Poulain's *Graces
of Interior Prayer*, Part iv, 'Revelations and Visions'.

the same time: the second is the inward teaching that I have understood therein *afterward*: the third, all the whole Revelation from the beginning to the end which our Lord God of His goodness *bringeth oftentimes* freely to the sight of mine understanding. And these three are so oned, as to my understanding, that I cannot, nor may, dispart them.'[1]

An important question for each one of us to decide, affecting our attitude towards the *Revelations*, is, How are we to think of Julian's mental condition at the time she underwent these experiences? Some interesting explanations have been offered. Dr. Inge speaks of 'the state of hypnotism induced by gazing at the Crucifix'.[2] Miss Underhill says, 'That tendency to visualization which plays so large a part in our mental life, and is specially powerful in minds of artistic or creative cast, here came into play'.[3] Thouless, after referring to her illness, remarks, 'Then her normal mental life was weakened, and the scenes of the Passion with which meditation had stored her mind welled up to the surface of consciousness and presented themselves with hallucinatory vividness'.[4] Knowles affirms, 'The characteristics of this type, perhaps more common among women than men, are certain morbid conditions of body combined with a claim to have heard or seen supernatural manifestations'.[5] Miss Warrack thinks it was not unlikely that in Julian's weakness of body and exaltation of spirit 'some sort of *physical illusion* should be brought about by her prolonged gaze upon the Face of the Crucifix'. But she adds, 'By God sickness and illusion, as well as things evil, are "suffered" to come, and by Him Revelation is given according to sundry times in diverse manners'.[6]

[1] *Revelations*, Ch. LI.   [2] *Studies of English Mystics*, p. 57.
[3] *The Mystic Way*, p. 227.   [4] *Lady Julian*, p. 25.
[5] *The English Mystics*, p. 130.
[6] *Introduction*, p. xxxviii; see also Streeter and Appasamy's *The Sadhu*, '. . . we shall not be inclined to deny that Visions may be a genuine revelation of truth', p. 115. See, too, Poulain as above.

It will be seen that Miss Warrack boldly combines the extremes of interpretation, the natural and the supernatural: the earthly is made to serve the heavenly. To those who do not feel at liberty to shut God out of human experience, especially when He has something of value to impart—and that, after all, is the supreme test of any alleged revelation—this solution will probably be acceptable.

At the time of Julian's First Revelation, when she saw the red blood trickle from under the Garland, she had also another kind of vision—'a spiritual sight of God's homely loving':

'He shewed me a little thing, the quantity of an hazel-nut, in the palm of my hand: and it was as round as a ball. I looked thereupon with the eye of my understanding, and thought: "What may this be?" And it was answered generally thus: "It is all that is made". I marvelled how it might last, for methought it might suddenly have fallen to naught for littleness. And I was answered in my understanding: "It lasteth, and ever shall last for God loveth it". And so All-thing hath the Being of God.'

'In this Little Thing I saw three properties. The first is that God made it, the second is that God loveth it, and the third that God keepeth it.'[1]

This spiritual intuition was given to Julian for her instruction, 'to teach her soul wisely to cleave to the Goodness of God'. We are not surprised that Julian was advised on the threshold of her experiences to cling to that cardinal fact—to be the central light of all her seeing—because almost at once she was to face the haunting problem of her book: the existence of evil.

The presence of evil—of sin, sorrow, and pain—in God's creation, is an agelong problem. The lovers and defenders of the Christian Faith have never tried to run away from it. Many solutions have been offered, but none for long have

[1] *Revelations*, Ch. V.

proved completely satisfying. The problem presses heavily upon the mystics, because it casts a dark shadow over their most cherished belief—the Divine Goodness. God to them is the Beloved of the soul, who willed a fair and beautiful world for the abode of His chosen; and who still desires, in spite of lurking shadows, that they shall enjoy all the good He can give. There is an unconscious tinge of Monism in most mystical thought.[1]   In the presence of this perplexing difficulty Julian displays an unwavering faith, a firm courage, and a daring speculation.

The problem was first presented to her in an intellectual vision:

'After this I saw God in a Point, that is to say, in mine understanding—by which sight I saw that He is in all things. I beheld and considered, seeing and knowing in sight, with a soft dread, and thought: "What is sin?" For I saw truly that God doeth all-thing, be it never so little. . . . And I was certain that He doeth no sin. And here I saw verily that sin is no deed; for in all this was not sin showed.'[2]

At once we are ready to assume that Julian was about to succumb to the great temptation of the mystically-minded: to accommodate her creed to her desire: to deny the reality of sin in the interests of the Divine Goodness. But in the soul of Julian there was a deep reverence for truth which would not let her knowingly be guilty of intellectual chicanery.   She allows us to listen to her musings:

'And I saw that nothing letted me but sin. And so I looked, generally, upon us all, and methought: "If sin had not been, we should all have been clean and like to our Lord, as He made us." And thus, in my folly, afore this time I wondered why by the great foreseeing wisdom of God the beginning of sin was not letted: for then, methought, all should have been well.'[3]

[1] See Sorley's *Moral Values and the Idea of God*, pp. 398 f.
[2] *Revelations*, Ch. XI.   [3] Ch. XXVII.

To this wistful longing she received a remarkable locution; it is the most famous saying in her book, and has
excited endless discussion. Some have labelled it rank
heresy; others see in it sublime faith:

'It behoved that there should be sin: but all shall be well,
and all shall be well, and all manner of thing shall be well.'[1]

Having received this message she proceeds to define sin
in a way to rob it of all actuality:

'In this naked word *sin*, our Lord brought to my mind,
generally, *all that is not good*, and the shameful despite and the
utter noughting that He bare for us in this life, and His dying:
and all the pains and passions of all His creatures, ghostly and
bodily. . . . But I saw not *sin*: for I believe it hath no manner
of substance nor no part of being, nor could it be known but
by the pain it is cause of.'[2]

She could not rest in this conclusion long; very soon
she is wrestling with the problem again:

'I stood beholding things general, troublously and mourn-
ing, saying thus to our Lord in my meaning, with full great
dread: "Ah! good Lord, how might all be well, for the great
hurt that is come, by sin, to the creature?" And here I
desired, as far as I durst, to have some more open declaring
wherewith I might be eased in this matter.'[3]

Her wish is granted; a ray of light penetrates the darkness. The blessed Lord answers that Adam's sin was the
most harm that ever was done, or ever shall be, to the
world's end; but she should behold the glorious Satisfaction,[4] which is more pleasing to God and more worshipful
than ever was the sin of Adam harmful. Hence,

'. . . since I have made well the most harm, then it is My
will that thou know thereby that I shall make well all that is
less'.[5]

Even though she finds that the facts of life, her own
experience, and the Divine voice compel the recognition

---

[1] Ch. XXVII.   [2] Ch. XXVII.   [3] Ch. XXIX.
[4] i.e. the Atonement.   [5] Ch. XXIX.

of sin, Julian is not yet completely ready to capitulate.
She now turns to a metaphysical doctrine of the will for
aid; she uses this to try and banish evil to some subsidiary
sphere of being:

'For in every soul that shall be saved is a Godly Will that
never assented to sin, nor ever shall. Right as there is a
beastly will in the lower part that may will no good, right so
there is a Godly Will in the higher part, which will is so good
that it may never will evil, but ever good.'[1]

In the after years of meditation, when Julian feels her
way further into this problem, she finds that this explanation is too facile. Not only is sin too real to be denied,
but its devastating effects are too universal to be confined
to a subordinate place, either in man's soul, or in the
general life of the world. Moreover, she awakens fully to
the fact that to regard sin as illusory brings her into conflict with the common teaching of Holy Church. What
shall she do? She plunges more deeply into the question.
She tosses it endlessly to and fro in her mind. But light
will not come. She grows anxious, distressed, fearful:
what agitation is revealed in such a broken question as
this:

'If I take it thus that we be no sinners and not blameworthy,
it seemeth that I should err and fail of knowing of this truth:
and if it be that we be sinners and blameworthy—Good
Lord, how may it then be that I cannot see this true thing in
Thee, which art my God, my Maker, in whom I desire to see
all truths?'[2]

Then at last she exclaims:

'And when we by Mercy of God and with His help accord
us to Nature and Grace, we shall see verily that sin is in sooth
viler and more painful than hell, without likeness; for it is
contrary to our fair nature. For as verily as sin is unclean, so
verily it is unnatural, and thus an horrible thing to see for the

[1] Ch. XXXVII.   [2] Ch. L.

loved soul that would be all fair and shining in the sight of
God, as Nature and Grace teacheth.

'Yet be we not adread of this, save inasmuch as dread may
speed us; but meekly make we our moan to our dear worthy
Mother, and He shall besprinkle us in His precious blood and
make our soul full soft and full mild, and heal us full fair by
process of time, right as it is most worship to Him and joy to
us without end. And of this sweet fair working He shall never
cease nor stint till all His dearworthy children be born and
forthbrought.'[1]

We ought to observe that while Julian was toying with
the notion that sin was 'without substance or being', she
was at the same time, contradictory though it may seem,
trying to give reasons for its existence. For instance, the
pain caused by sin purges us, makes us to know ourselves,
and to ask God's mercy;[2] sin is the sharpest scourge that
any soul may be smitten with—but for the healing of these
wounds it is driven into the life of Holy Church;[3] God
allows us to be blamed and despised in this world—
scorned, mocked, and outcasted—that we may be saved
from the pomp and vain-glory of this wretched life.[4] But
there was a deeper purpose than any of these. Christ
would overcome man's sin by His glorious Satisfaction,
and in doing so should bring such honour and praise to
God as would not be possible in any other way. This will
be made finally clear on a Great Day, known only to our
blessed Lord:

'And the cause why He willeth that we know this Deed shall
be, is for that He would have us the more eased in our soul
and the more set at peace in love—leaving the beholding of all
troublous things that might keep us back from true enjoying
of Him. This is that Great Deed . . . by which He shall make
all things well.'[5]

In this connexion we can best consider another daring
statement by this questing Saint. In heaven, by the power

[1] Ch. LXIII.   [2] Ch. XXVII.   [3] Ch. XXXIX.
[4] Ch. XXVII.   [5] Ch. XXXII.

of God, a wonderful transmutation is wrought: sin is turned into honour, woes into joy, and wounds into honourable scars. This is the reward of those who, while they failed in some of their trials and temptations, kept a sincere intention throughout, showed deep contrition for their failures, and in the end proved themselves faithful. Heaven welcomes these as warriors. Julian mentions Biblical characters like David and Mary Magdalene, and historical persons like St. John of Beverley,

'And others also without number: how they are known in the Church in earth with their sins, and it is to them no shame, but all is turned for them to worship.'[1]

Lest some might imagine from this that it paid to do evil—'Shall we continue in sin that grace may abound?'—Julian hastens to correct that assumption. In her grave warning we see both her true estimate of sin and her essential sanity:

'I am sure by my own feeling, the more that any kind soul seeth this in the courteous love of our Lord God, the lother he is to sin and the more he is ashamed. For if afore us were laid together all the pains in Hell and in Purgatory and in Earth —death and other—and by itself sin, we should rather choose all that pain than sin. For sin is so vile and so greatly to be hated that it may be likened to no pain which is not sin. For a kind soul hath no hell but sin.'[2]

Some cannot escape the awful penalty of their deeds and neglect (though we wish she could have excepted the 'heathen' from this punishment, and so broken away from the hard tradition of that age),

'as angels that fell out of heaven for pride, which be now fiends: and man in earth that dieth out of the Faith of Holy Church; that is to say, they that be heathen men: and also man that hath received christendom and liveth unchristian life and so dieth out of charity; all these shall be condemned to hell without end, as Holy Church teacheth me to believe'.[3]

[1] Ch. XXXVIII.   [2] Ch. XL.   [3] Ch. XXXII.

When, however, we read that, we feel bound to turn to another passage: one of the most beloved and celebrated in her book:

'The dearworthy blood of our Lord Jesus Christ as verily as it is most precious, so verily it is most plenteous. Behold and see! The precious plenty of His dearworthy blood descended down into Hell and burst her bands and delivered all that were there which belonged to the Court of Heaven. The precious plenty of His dearworthy blood overfloweth all Earth, and is ready to wash all creatures of sin, which be of goodwill, have been, and shall be. The precious plenty of His dearworthy blood ascended up into Heaven to the blessed body of our Lord Jesus Christ, and there is in Him, bleeding and praying to the Father—and is, and shall be as long as it needeth—and ever shall be as long as it needeth. And evermore it floweth in all Heavens enjoying the salvation of all mankind, that are there, and shall be—fulfilling the number that faileth.'[1-2]

Another important subject dealt with by Julian is Prayer. Here we shall see that she was far in advance of her age. Her words make it apparent that she was critical of certain habits of devotion which had crept into the Church and were threatening the purity of its worship and doctrine. She is particularly impatient of 'means'; these she roundly condemns for their 'lack of understanding and knowing of love'. The means she specifies are such as: Christ's holy flesh and precious blood, His holy Passion, His Mother's love, and intercession to special saints. All these, Julian emphasizes, for any efficacy they may have, are dependent upon the Divine Goodness; therefore it is better that appeal be made direct to God.

'For as the body is clad in the cloth, and the flesh in the skin, and the bones in the flesh, and the heart in the whole, so are we, soul and body, clad in the Goodness of God, and enclosed.'[3]

Even more modern is the teaching of the Fourteenth

[1] i.e. the appointed number of heavenly citizens.
[2] Ch. XII.   [3] Ch. VI.

Revelation. This is entirely given over to the subject of Prayer and contains some of her profoundest thought. She begins the chapter by confessing that in her approaches to God she is sometimes conscious of unworthiness, and of barrenness and dryness both before and after her devotions. Then comes this remarkable locution:

'I am the Ground of thy beseeching; first it is my will that thou have it: and after, I make thee to will it: and after, I make thee to beseech it and thou beseechest it. How should it then be that thou shouldst not have thy beseeching?'[1]

Probably the philosophy of Prayer has never been more concisely stated than that. God is the *Ground*: Prayer begins, continues, and ends in Him: He is source, subject and fulfilment. Prayer of this kind cuts out everything selfish; the soul does not ask for special favours, least of all does it desire to bend the Divine will to its own. Every request will be conditioned by the qualification observed by the Master Himself: 'If it be Thy will'. When we come in this spirit, 'full glad and merry is the Lord of our prayer'; and we shall find that, though offered in dryness and barrenness, in sadness and feebleness, it will be well-pleasing in His sight: 'God accepts the will and the travail of His servant, however we feel.'

Moreover, prayer of this nature achieves its true purpose: it unites us to God, and in that union we find our soul's perfect satisfaction. Julian's words on this point are comprehensive and beautiful; to express the soul's fulness of joy, she uses the five senses as symbols of our spiritual perceptions:

'Prayer oneth the soul to God. . . . And well I wot, the more the soul seeth of God, the more it desireth Him by His grace. . . . And then shall we, with His sweet grace, in our own meek continuant prayer come unto Him now in this life by many privy touchings of sweet spiritual sights and feeling, measured to us as our simpleness may bear it. And this is

[1] Ch. XLI.

wrought, and shall be, by the grace of the Holy Ghost, so long that we die in longing, for love. And then shall we all come into our Lord, our Self clearly knowing, and God fully having: and we shall endlessly be all had in God; Him verily seeing and fully feeling, Him spiritually hearing, and delectably in-breathing, and of Him sweetly drinking. And then shall we see God face to face, homely and fully.'[1]

Julian accepts the Seven Sacraments of the Church, 'each following other in order as God hath ordained them'; but she has little to say about them. She mentions three: confession, penance, and the eucharist. She casually recommends the first two; though in reference to the first, there was a special occasion when she would like to have been shriven, but she felt the priest would not believe her confession. To the third she makes a more intimate allusion: '. . . the Blessed Sacrament that is precious food of my life'.[2] From this it would appear that Julian obtained special benefit from the Service of the Altar; it may be, not only when she was communicating, but when she followed the service from her little window looking into the sanctuary. She nowhere makes any comment to indicate interest in transubstantiation; her references might have been made by any good evangelical.

How much Julian read, what books she studied, who, among the great writers were her favourite teachers, we cannot tell. That she read deeply and selectively is clear from many a page of her book. Probably the authors who contributed most to her education, mental and spiritual, were the same as those of her predecessors: the later Church Fathers, the medieval ascetical writers, and some of the Scholastics. Many traces reveal her appreciation of her fellow-English mystics: her warm celebrations of the Divine Love recall the ecstasies of the Yorkshire hermit; and her reasonings about the soul remind us of Walter Hilton. Hilton and Julian have one pregnant

[1] Ch. XLIII.   [2] Ch. LX.

sentence in common: 'our soul is a life'; but which was indebted to the other it is impossible to say. The wealth of pictorial and descriptive matter in her visions and parables indicates that Julian had given no small attention to the beautiful art products of the East Anglian school. From these varied sources Julian gathers choicest treasures which she built into the framework of her own individuality. The result is one of the most original, forceful, and lovable characters we know, with a unique experience to relate, and able to tell it in a way that captivates our mind and heart.

In her spiritual ascent Julian favoured the open and upward way. She never hints at macerations; her ascetical practices seem to have been limited to those recommended in the New Testament: prayer, fasting, and almsgiving. She knew the methods of the *via negativa*, and now and again, in the interests of concentrated effort, was ready to adopt them.[1] But we hear little from her of the Divine Darkness or the Dark Night of the Soul. This does not mean that she knew nothing of darkness. She often laments her liability to the besetting sins of the solitary life: indolence, sloth, doubtful dread, and bitter despair; but these were only passing phases of the soul's life. Before long she emerged into the sunshine. As showing how essentially healthy-minded Julian was, Miss Warrack can say, 'Julian's mystical sight was not a negation of human modes of thought; neither was it a torture to human powers of speech; nor a death-sentence to human activities of feeling'.[2] Hence, Julian can claim, as her supreme reward, to be 'highly lifted up into contemplation by the special gift of our Lord';[3] and she can define this contemplation as being the 'inward beholding of His blessed Goodness',[4] in which she is 'oned to God'.

Julian was more metaphysical than the other English mystics. A few examples will illustrate this, and, at the same time, throw some light on her learning and culture.

[1] Ch. V.   [2] 'Introduction', p. xl.   [3] Ch. LXXVIII.   [4] Ch. LXXVI.

Writing of the Divine Being she says, 'I saw God in a Point';[1] 'He is the Mid-point of all thing, and all He doeth';[2] 'He is the ground, He is the substance, He is the same thing that is Nature-hood'.[3] Of man she writes, 'For we are all double by God's making: that is to say, Substantial and Sensual'[4]—the former is the higher self and centres in God, the latter is the sense-soul and inhabits the body on earth. We also have two wills: 'the Godly Will' that never assents to sin, and 'the beastly will' that can will no good.[5] Of ethics she says, 'For the life and virtue that we have in the lower part is of the higher, and it cometh down to us from out of the Natural love of the high Self, by the working of grace'.[6] In her treatment of the Trinity she is specially versatile and profound, and here Neoplatonic influence can be traced.

Some other striking differences are noticed between Julian and her fellow-English mystics. There is the Bible: Julian frequently acknowledges her debt to Holy Scripture, and accepts it as the fountain of Truth; but, unlike her predecessors, she seldom quotes it—throughout her book there are only three short texts. There is allegory: other mystical writers make lavish use of this time-honoured method, especially when they use Biblical characters and events to illustrate their teaching, but this style of writing and reasoning is almost absent from Julian. Then there is lechery: to other saints this vice had become a haunting dread; it is not so much as mentioned in Julian's book.

We have already referred to Julian's humility; it is one of her most appealing traits. Scattered about her pages are confessions like this:

'For truly it was not shewed me that God loved me better than the least soul that is in grace: for I am certain that there be many that never had shewing nor sight but of the common teaching of Holy Church, that love God better than I.'[7]

[1] Ch. XI.   [2] Ch. XI.   [3] Ch. LXII.   [4] Ch. LVIII.
[5] Ch. XXXVII.   [6] Ch. LII.   [7] Ch. IX.

That was not a pose: on page after page of her book the same spirit is manifest. In order to disclaim any appearance of dogmatism, she often qualifies her sayings with the phrase, 'as to my sight'; this becomes one of the endearing touches of her book. On one particular occasion, she greatly desired a 'singular Shewing' as to whether a friend, whom she greatly loved, would continue to grow in grace. Before long she is stricken with remorse for asking this *special* favour: 'For the fulness of joy is to behold God in all';[1] hence her constant emphasis on her relationship to, and equality with, her 'even-Christians'. The same spirit comes out in her attitude towards Holy Church. She points out that there are two manner of beholdings: one in her revelations, and the other in the teaching of the Church. If these two clash, which is she to accept? When faced with this dilemma her *naïveté* is delightful. She fully states what she has been taught in her vision, then she hastens to add that she must be mindful of what she learnt from Mother Church![2] Julian's humility is so natural that she would see nothing incongruous in this.

Considering that Julian wrote when the vernacular was still in its early stages, it is astonishing what masterly use she makes of it. For the most part her writing resembles a moorland stream flowing gently along with crystalline clearness and a sweet musical murmur. That figure, however, is not a complete representation of her style. Other aspects at times seize our admiration: little idiosyncrasies of expression which give it picturesqueness and charm; graphic elements which make it vital and vivid— imparting to the imagery life and movement. There are occasions, too, when her prose becomes poetry—this is when she describes her soul's joy in apprehension of Divine Love or in contemplation of Eternal Truth.

From this it will be gathered that Julian easily turns to figures of speech; their variety and range are surprising.

[1] Ch. XXXV.   [2] Ch. XLVI.

One striking instance is when she recalls her vision of the crucifix, and she saw the blood starting from beneath the garland of thorns:

'These three came to my mind in the time; pellots, for roundness, in the coming out of the blood: the scale of herring, in the spreading on the forehead: the drops off the eaves, for the plenteousness innumerable.'[1] Another instance is when she describes the appearance of the flesh of the face and body as 'small-rimpled with a tanned colour, like a dry board when it is aged'.[2] And still another, of a different kind, is when she refers to the sufferings of her even-Christians: 'For God's servants, Holy Church, shall be shaken in sorrow and anguish, tribulation in this world, as men shake a cloth in a wind.'[3]

She likes to present truth parabolically; this gives free play to her originality. Here are two brief examples. She gives the first after reasoning about God's power to keep the soul in peace and safety; the second, containing the element of glad surprise, illustrates the purity of the soul when rising from its sinful body:

'One time mine understanding was led down into the sea-ground, and there I saw hills and dales green, seeming as it were moss-be-grown, with wrack and gravel.'[4]

'And in this time I saw a body lying on the earth, which body shewed heavy and horrible, without shape and form, as it were a swollen quag of stinking mire. And suddenly out of this body sprang a full fair creature, a little Child, fully shapen and formed, nimble and lively, whiter than lily: which swiftly glided up into heaven.'[5]

She has many similar 'bodily examples' as she calls them; some of them are long illustrations very cleverly worked out in detail, seeking to convey not only moral and spiritual truth, but also theological and metaphysical facts. One of the best known is that of the Lord and the Servant, in which God, Adam, and Christ are discussed in relationship to the Fall, the Incarnation, and the redemp-

[1] Ch. VII. [2] Ch. XVII. [3] Ch. XXVIII. [4] Ch. X. [5] Ch. LXIV.

tion of mankind; and attempts are made to solve the problems of the origin and nature, the guilt and punishment of sin.[1]

Epigrams and apothegms are lavishly scattered over her pages. Some of them are unforgettable: they concentrate all her excellences—her chaste thought, swift intuition, sweet modesty, spiritual devotion, and charm of literary expression:

'God is all that is good, as to my sight, and the goodness that each thing hath, it is He.'[2]

'And thus I saw Him, and sought Him: and I had Him, and I wanted Him.'[3]

'And then I saw that each kind compassion that a man hath on his even-Christians with charity, it is Christ in him.'[4]

'Truth seeth God, and Wisdom beholdeth God, and of these two cometh the third; that is, a holy marvellous delight in God: which is Love.'[5]

'For right as by the courtesy of God He forgiveth our sin after the time that we repent us, right so willeth He that *we* forgive our sin, as anent our unskilful heaviness and our doubtful dreads.'[6]

'Flee we to our Lord and we shall be comforted, touch we Him and we shall be made clean, cleave we to Him and we shall be sure, and safe from all manner of peril.'[7]

Julian's closing words to her book shall be ours to this chapter:

'And from that time that it was shewed I desired oftentimes to learn what was our Lord's meaning. And fifteen years after, and more, I was answered in ghostly understanding, saying thus; "Wouldst thou learn thy Lord's meaning in this thing? Learn it well; Love was His meaning. Who shewed it thee? Love. What shewed He thee? Love. Wherefore shewed it He? For Love. Hold thee therein and thou shalt learn and know more in the same. But thou shalt never know nor learn therein other thing without end." Thus was I learned that Love was our Lord's meaning.'[8]

[1] Ch. LI.   [2] Ch. VIII.   [3] Ch. X.   [4] Ch. XXVIII.   [5] Ch. XLIV.
[6] Ch. LXXIII.   [7] Ch. LXXVI.   [8] Ch. LXXXVI.

CHAPTER VIII

MARGERY KEMPE

THE recent discovery of *The Book of Margery Kempe* brings welcome treasure to the World of Letters, and adds a romantic chapter to the story of English Literature. The existence of the book had long been suspected. In the University Library of Cambridge, there is a tiny quarto of eight pages, printed by Wynkyn de Worde (*c.* 1501), which opens with the words, 'Here begynneth a shorte treatyse of contemplacyon taught by our Lorde Jhesu Cryste, or taken out of the Boke of Margerie Kempe of Lynn'.[1] With a few insignificant variations, this tract was reprinted twenty years later by Pepwell (*c.* 1521). So far as we know this precious little volume of contemplation had not again been published till it was included by the late Professor Edmund G. Gardner in his scholarly collection of English mystical writings, *The Cell of Self-Knowledge*; and of it he wrote, 'No manuscript of the work is known to exist, and absolutely no traces can be discovered of the *Book of Margery Kempe*, out of which it is implied by the Printer that these beautiful thoughts and sayings are taken'.[2] Gardner evidently went to some trouble to try and establish the identity of Margery Kempe, and he thought he had found this 'mysterious personage' in an ancress of the same name who lived towards the end of the thirteenth century. His tentative conclusion is now proved to have been mistaken.

The story of the finding of the manuscript makes

---

[1] *The Cell of Self-Knowledge*, p. xix. [2] p. xx.

fascinating reading. From a note on its fly-leaf we learn that it was for a time in the possession of the Carthusian monks of Mount Grace Priory, near Northallerton. Since the Reformation, this once splendid and famous House has been a ruin. From the numerous marginal notes and sketches on the pages of the manuscript, it is evident that the monks had a loving regard for this devotional work. After being lost for five centuries, it came to light three years ago, in the library of Pleasington Old Hall, Lancashire, owned by Lieutenant-Colonel W. Butler-Bowdon, who tells us how he thinks it got there:

'It may be remembered that we are a Catholic family and I believe that, when the monasteries were being destroyed, the monks sometimes gave valuable books, vestments, &c., to such families in the hope of preserving them. Though there is nothing to prove it, this may have been the case with Margery Kempe's manuscript, and the Carthusians of Mount Grace may have given it to one of my family. . . . We used to look at it occasionally and sometimes visitors read a page or two of it. . . . It was shown to Miss Hope Emily Allen who identified it as Margery Kempe's lost autobiography.'[1]

The 'Book' now placed before us is the longer form of two versions. It is exactly dated: the first part was completed in 1436, and the second in 1438. For the writing of this larger work, Margery had secured the services of a priest, and she gave him her fullest help. She tells us, too, that she and her scribe made use of an earlier and shorter copy produced in 1432. Prior to that date Margery had been searching a long time for some one to take down her words, but had not succeeded in finding a suitable person. Then she became friendly with an Englishman, who had lived in Dewcheland, and had returned to this country. She made him her amanuensis. Residence abroad, however, must have affected his ability to express himself in his native language. Margery complains that 'he could

---

[1] *The Times*, Sept. 30, 1936.

neither well write English nor Duch'. Hence when the priest came to transcribe this copy, he needed not only Margery's assistance, but also divine illumination; with this heavenly help he was able to master the crabbed style and ill-written script. He added at the same time, at Margery's dictation, a considerable amount of new matter.

Margery's unique story has had a wonderful reception. It enjoyed the distinction of being heralded by special articles in *The Times*, including a laudatory leading article. Other accredited journals greeted it as the most interesting literary find of the present age. Of all unforeseen possibilities, a mystical work proved to be one of the season's best-sellers! It has made an instantaneous appeal to numerous circles. Scholars specially interested in the evolution of our mother tongue, have welcomed it as an excellent specimen of Middle English which will prove of immense help in their investigations. One of the experts of this group, Professor R. W. Chambers, who wrote the Introduction to the present edition,[1] describes it enthusiastically as an 'exceptional document', and confidently makes for it the claim 'to be the first extant biography in the English tongue'. Students of mysticism have hailed it with similar gratitude. As an intimate record of personal religious experience it has few equals. The marks of accuracy, sincerity, and reality are stamped on every page. It is sure to leap to the front rank of those confessional biographies so much valued as helps to holy living. Those devoted to medical and surgical subjects will find much to excite their interest in the quaint descriptions of certain forms of disease, and the methods of treatment. As for psychologists and psycho-analysts, they will find in these frank and full reminiscences a 'case' after their own heart; though one trembles to think what will happen to poor

[1] *The Book of Margery Kempe*, modern version by W. Butler-Bowdon. (Jonathan Cape.)

Margery when these cold-blooded dissectors really get to work! To the general public the volume will appeal mainly as an entrancing travel-story. Margery conducts us along some of the most frequented pilgrim-routes of this country, the Continent, and the Holy Land. She introduces us to a wide variety of human types, lighting up their characters with inimitable touches; and she lets us listen first-hand to their conversation, which is freely spiced with native wit and broad humour. As giving a picture of the medieval scene the book is invaluable. It will make an admirable companion volume to that other rare collection of medieval documents, *The Paston Letters*.

Margery's name is mentioned only once in the book. She consistently refers to herself as 'this creature'. This expression marks her humility, and indicates her acute sense of personal weakness and unworthiness in contrast to the majesty and glory of the Creator. She is ruthless in the delineation of her own character. She hides nothing; mitigates and extenuates nothing; and, except from God, asks neither mercy nor pity. She repeatedly stigmatizes herself as a 'sinful caitif' and a 'vile wretch'; but we feel that Margery, in this utter self-abasement, is doing what many other saints have done: to magnify the grace of God they vilify themselves. On the other hand, also like other saints, she claims and displays marvellous powers, whose operations produce in her body and mind extraordinary results, which at times are most alarming. She is sure to be variously labelled as eccentric, neurotic, or psychopathic; but none of these terms will explain her. Margery's personality is bound to puzzle many, especially if they are unfamiliar with certain mystical types, to be found mostly amongst ancresses and nuns.

One side of her nature—the practical—will present no difficulty; though even here Margery is far from normal. She was a devout lover of God's house, and, if they were worthy, of its ministrants; its numerous services also played a large part in her life. Her appreciation of symbolic values made her susceptible to crucifixes, images, pictures, ornaments, and altar lights. At the elevation of the Host she would bow in breathless adoration. She leaned hard on her confessors; gladly accepted their directions; and, because it gave her a sense of security, sought frequently to be shriven. She practised the most rigorous ascetic exercises in the spirit of an athlete. Pilgrimages took up much of her time; she never grew tired of visiting sacred shrines, holy relics, and hermits and ancresses. Two of her chief joys were to listen to the reading of Scripture, and to sermons; she would walk miles to hear a good preacher. She was touchingly tender-hearted, and generous, some might think, to the point of folly. To the poor, sick, aged, and infirm, she was an unfailing friend. All weak and wounded creatures, human or animal, instantly excited her pity; in some mystical manner they shared the Cross:

'And sometimes, when she saw the crucifix, or if she saw a man with a wound, or a beast, whichever it were, or if a man beat a child before her, or smote a horse or other beast with a whip, if she saw it or heard it, she thought she saw Our Lord being beaten or wounded, just as she saw it in the man or beast either in the field or the town.'[1]

When necessary she could be painfully outspoken: ecclesiastics and aristocrats of all ranks, civic dignitaries, and members of the more lowly classes, had all smarted from the lash of her tongue. Her evangelical zeàl sometimes bordered upon fanaticism; she would not let people alone; her caustic speech and persistent interference got her into endless trouble. But Margery was never one to 'take care'. She was brave in the face of danger, patient in suffering, and ready to run risks for Christ's sake. She would have welcomed the martyr's crown.

But there was another side to her nature—she was

[1] p. 108.

highly psychical. This fact proved embarrassing to her contemporaries, and it may alienate not a few of her readers to-day. In considering the phenomena associated with this condition, we must remember the age in which she lived. It was widely accepted that choice souls, wholly consecrated to the service of God, could, by the practice of the prayer-life, so mortify the powers of the body that the supernatural forces of the soul were released. By means of them it was possible to communicate with the unseen world. The doubt in the minds of Margery's fellow-believers was whether she was an elect soul or a hypocrite; the latter accusation was frequently flung at her. Her transports took on many forms. She enjoyed visions, locutions, and raptures; she could foretell the future; by specially directed prayer she could cure the sick, save life, and help a soul out of purgatory. There were more unusual forms. Wild outbursts of weeping would suddenly sweep from her; by the vehemence of her sobs, cries, and screams she frightened people. These paroxysms were at times more alarming. She would fling herself down like one demented: she would wrestle and rave, make horrible grimaces, and while her face turned as livid as lead, sweat would pour from her. Her sex-consciousness was rendered highly abnormal; even in old age she was haunted with the dread of defilement. Her discussions with her husband as to their taking vows of chastity, her debate with herself and others as to whether she should wear white clothes, and her suspicion and fear of practically every man she met, were all manifestations of the same sex aberration. On the other hand, the records of her supernatural communications with the heavenly world—with Christ, the Virgin, and the Saints —are so chaste, familiar, and realistic, as to move the heart of the reader profoundly. In her conversations with our Lord, she approaches Him at different times as her Friend, Bridegroom, and Husband, but never once are these intimate exchanges marred by any element of eroticism: they are kept on the loftiest plane. Long passages of the biography are occupied with meditations of this kind: they are some of the choicest in the whole range of devotional literature.

It will be clearly understood that these two aspects of Margery's personality—the practical and the psychical—are neither contradictory nor irreconcileable; of course, they cannot be separated: each penetrates the other. In a number of mystics, particularly women, they have produced characters of extraordinary force and beauty. So with Margery. Her unconventional mode of life and behaviour was often misrepresented and misunderstood; she had to endure much scurrilous gossip and cruel opposition; people whose friendship she sought boycotted her; priests would not shrive her; preachers banned her from their congregations; yet she remained a lovable tender-hearted woman. That is why she could also claim hosts of friends. In grace of character, arduousness of life, triumphant faith, and contempt of death, she bears comparison with her great contemporaries: St. Bridget of Sweden, St. Catherine of Sienna, and St. Joan of Arc.

Margery Kempe was born at the large and busy port of Lynn in 1373. Her father was John of Brunham, five times Mayor of Lynn, and Alderman of the High Guild of the Trinity. When about twenty years old, she married John Kempe, a worshipful burgess of Lynn, to whom she bore fourteen children. After the birth of the first baby her mind for a time was unhinged. 'She was wondrously vexed and laboured with spirits for half a year, eight weeks, and odd days.' The devils threatened and taunted her, and bade her forsake the Christian Faith. She was released from this madness by a vision of the Saviour.

'He appeared in the likeness of a man, most seemly, most beauteous and most amiable that ever might be seen with man's eye, clad in a mantle of purple silk, sitting upon her bedside, looking upon her with so blessed a face that she was strengthened in all her spirit, and said to her these words; "Daughter, why hast thou forsaken Me, and I forsook never thee?" And anon, as He said these words, she saw verily how the air opened as bright as any lightning. And He rose up into the air, not right hastily and quickly, but fair and easily, so that she might well behold Him in the air till it was closed again.'[1]

The transforming spiritual change, however, had not yet come. The world and its ways still gripped her. Pride in dress and ornaments, no matter how extravagant the fashions, was her weakness.

'She wore gold pipes on her head, and her hoods, with the tippets, were slashed. Her cloaks also were slashed, so that they should be the more staring to men's sight, and herself the more worshipped.'[2]

To maintain these vanities she had to set about getting more money. With characteristic spirit she became a brewer, and later, a miller; at both she failed dismally. This badly shook her confidence; she interpreted it as a sign of divine displeasure. Now her thoughts seriously turned Godwards. The fact is worth noting that when the call did come its form was not unlike that of Richard Rolle's. One night, as she lay in bed,

'she heard a sound of melody so sweet and delectable, that she thought she had been in Paradise, and therewith she started out of her bed and said; "Alas that ever I did sin ! It is full merry in Heaven". This melody was so sweet that it surpassed all melody that ever might be heard in this world, without any comparison, and caused her, when she heard any mirth or melody afterwards, to have full plenteous and abundant tears of high devotion, with great sobbings and sighings after the bliss of Heaven, not dreading the shames and spites of this wretched world'.[3]

That night Margery passed from darkness into light; the

[1] p. 25.   [2] p. 27.   [3] p. 30.

interior revolution had come; she was a new woman. That was also the first time she experienced the 'gift of tears' which, for the rest of her life, was to be both a blessing and a bane. Very soon Margery was well-set on 'the way of high perfection'. She determined to pursue it steadfastly to its goal—complete consecration to Christ and His service.

One of her first reactions was a heightened sense of sex. Speaking of her earlier marriage-relations with her husband, she confesses, in her direct way, that 'in her young age, she had full many delectable thoughts, fleshly lusts, and inordinate loves to his person'.[1] Those pleasures had now become repugnant, even their memory was a pain. No novice ever embraced the vow of perpetual virginity with greater ardour than Margery would have done if only she could. She will do the next best thing: though a wife, she will live as a virgin. She begs of her husband to take with her a vow of chastity. But John, kind, considerate, and longsuffering though he is, is not yet prepared to enter into this pact. But 'three or four years after', Margery had the immense satisfaction of securing his agreement. While travelling from York to Bridlington on a hot summer's day they stopped to rest beneath a cross in a field. There John made a definite offer. If Margery would pay his debts before she went to Jerusalem, and would no longer observe Friday as a fast day, he would consent. Margery found the second condition hard to accept; but after praying beneath the cross for heavenly guidance, she said,

'Sir, if it please you, ye shall grant me my desire, and ye shall have your desire. Grant me that ye will not come into my bed, and I grant you to requite your debts ere I go to Jerusalem. Make my body free to God so that ye never make challenge to me, by asking any debt of matrimony. After this

[1] p. 266.

day, whilst ye live, I will eat and drink on Friday at your bidding. Then said her husband, "As free may your body be to God, as it hath been to me".[1]

Margery and John now set out to visit certain holy shrines. Their experience at Canterbury may be accepted as an illustration of what happened at many other places. Margery, 'because she wept so fast', got into trouble with monks, priests, and secular men. When she quietly thanked them for their contempt, they grew enraged, and cried, 'Thou shalt be burnt, false Lollard. Here is a cartful of thorns ready for thee, and a tun to burn thee with'.[2] When she was quaking with fear, two fair young men came to her rescue and took her safely to the hostel where her husband was staying.

The Lollards, as early Reformers, were regarded by most of those in authority as heretics and revolutionaries, and given an evil reputation. Because of her irregular manner of life, her long journeys alone to distant parts of the country, her lack of deference to the official classes, and, most of all, the malicious rumours current concerning her, she was often taken for a Lollard, and her life was in danger.

Margery now began to prepare for one of her greatest adventures—the journey to the Holy Land. When, by divine revelation, she was informed that she should undertake this pilgrimage, she was told she must wear white clothes. Before adopting this distinctive dress, she thought it wise to secure episcopal approval. For this purpose she sought an interview with Philip Repington, Bishop of Lincoln, one of the foremost ecclesiastics of his day. She said,

'My lord, if it pleases you, I am commanded in my soul that ye should give me the mantle and ring, and clothe me in white clothes'.[3]

[1] p. 49.   [2] p. 55.   [3] p. 60.

Her husband expressed his willingness that his wife's
desire should be gratified. The Bishop, however, after
consultation with learned clerks, had, for the time being,
to withhold his approval. Very kindly, he said, 'My
counsel will not allow me to profess you in such singular
clothing, without better advice'. He suggested, as she
was not in his diocese, that she should go and ask leave
of Arundel, Archbishop of Canterbury. On arrival at
Lambeth, she was invited to talk with the Archbishop in
his garden; but the only request she made was that he
would give her permission, under his letter and seal, to
choose her confessor and be houselled every Sunday
wherever she might be, if God should dispose her thereto.
This was readily granted. Then Margery spent a gracious
time telling him of her manner of life. Her concluding
note upon the interview has a touch of poetry: 'And so
their dalliance continued till stars appeared in the
firmament.'

About this time Margery was sorely troubled by persistent opposition and cruel slanders. They led to keen
self-examination. Could she be mistaken? Was it possible that her celestial revelations were illusions from
demoniac sources? She consulted numerous saintly and
learned persons, amongst them Dame Julian of Norwich,
'for the anchoress was expert in such things, and good
counsel could give'. Julian, with the soundness of insight
we should expect, was able to reassure Margery, telling
her that there were three sure tests of heavenly inspira-
tions: they would assist in the true worship of God, would
promote chasteness of soul, and would unseal tears of
contrition, devotion, and compassion. This report of
several days' heart-to-heart talks between these two remarkable women truly reflects, with one exception, the
character and style of Julian as we know them from her
Revelations. In Margery's account, Julian presses home
her points with quotations from Scripture; these, as

we have seen, are almost entirely absent from her own book.[1]

At last, in 1414, Margery set sail from Yarmouth for her long-contemplated visit to the Holy Land. At Zierikzee,[2] she got into trouble with her confessor and travelling companions because of her religious zeal. They strongly objected to her abstention from flesh and wine, her boisterous sobbings, and her constant talk about the love and goodness of God. Evidently her piety rebuked their laxity: it prevented them from having a good time! Chaucer's pilgrims made a similar complaint of one of their number. The bickerings continued on the way to Constance. There her companions tried to cure her by making her a laughing-stock:

'They cut down her gown so short that it came but little beneath her knee, and made her put on a white canvas, in the manner of a sacken apron, so that she should be held a fool and the people should not make much of her or hold her in repute.'[3]

They also forbade her to go with them any longer. In turning her adrift they kept back most of her money, and her maiden. She was brought by an old man to Bologna, where, on promising to amend her ways, she was allowed to rejoin the company. They stayed at Venice for thirteen weeks; here Margery could no longer bottle-up her enthusiasm, and quarrels again broke out.

In sailing to the Holy Land, Margery tried to avoid the rest of the company; but when they heard of this attempt, they deserted their ship, and insisted on going in hers. If she enjoyed divine protection they wanted to share it! Even then they could not leave her alone. 'And so she had ever much tribulation till she came to Jerusalem.' The sight of the Holy City banished her sorrows. She

[1] In another place, Margery also refers with gratitude to the works of Richard Rolle and Walter Hilton.
[2] A port in S.W. Holland. [3] Ibid., p. 98.

began at once the customary round of visits to the sacred places associated with the life and death of our Lord; but for the most part the record tells only of violent weepings. When we think of the mass of interesting facts upon which Margery's vivid pen could have reported, we deeply regret the meagre details she has preserved.

On the return journey Margery and her fellowship reached Venice in safety; there her countrymen forsook her, saying that they would not go with her any further for a hundred pounds. Margery had been inwardly instructed that she must proceed to Rome, and must wear white clothes. Her escort was a broken-backed man named Richard, a native of Ireland, a professional beggar, whose presence and help at such a moment of need had been foretold to her before she left England. On arrival at Rome she went about for the first time in white clothes. She had to endure much mockery, especially from women. Her other curious modes of behaviour—sobbings, loud cries, prolonged devotions, and interference with strangers —increased her enemies. At first she had to beg from door to door. Later many were attracted to her and offered her a home, not a few sought her spiritual ministrations, believing devoutly in her supernatural gifts. At this point her narrative is again alive with interest as she describes the various types of people she met, and the adventures she underwent. As usual she spent much time in visiting churches: for prayer and meditation, for the celebration of a notable Festival, or to hear a favourite preacher. As an act of penance, she served for six weeks an old woman living in dire poverty; Margery suffered much from cold, vermin, and scarcity of food. A compensating experience was the joy of meeting St. Bridget's maiden, and learning that the Saint 'was kind and meek to every creature, and that she had a laughing face'. By our Lord's command, she gave away in charity her own money and some borrowed from the broken-backed man;

but a short time after, a priest from England, also acting by divine commission, sought her out and gave her sufficient gold to return home.

When Margery and her fellowship set out from Rome they made for Middleburg.[1] Though they had been warned against robbers and murderers the journey was safely accomplished, their only distress coming from severe storms on land and sea. When she got home she found that during her absence calumny had been busy. An anchorite accused her of having had a child whilst she was abroad; with calm disdain she denied the scandal. In Norwich 'a good man' provided her with cloth 'for a gown, a hood, a kirtle and a cloak'. As in Rome, so in her native land, she had to suffer much abuse and scorn for going about in white raiment. Her husband sought her in Norwich and took her home to Lynn. Soon afterwards, perhaps owing to the rigours of her travels, she was afflicted with painful sickness which brought her to the point of death. At this time, too, her tearful outbursts became more fearsome than ever, and people ostracized her.

Two years after returning from Rome Margery was ready for another pilgrimage: to St. James of Compostella, in Spain. Funds came from unexpected quarters. At Bristol—as she had foretold—she met the broken-backed man and repaid him the money borrowed in Rome. During an unavoidable delay of six weeks, because 'the ships were arrested and taken up for the King', one of her hosts was Thomas Marchale of Newcastle, who became a worthy friend. Some who distrusted her compelled her to appear for examination before the Bishop of Worcester: as the kindly prelate knew Margery and her father well, the interview was full of profit to both parties. Circumstances now being favourable, Margery crossed to Spain; she was back within a month. Nothing noteworthy is recorded of her experiences.

[1] Another port in S.W. Holland.

Still pursuing her pious pastime of visiting sacred shrines, she next came, with Thomas Marchale as a companion, to Leicester. Here, after weeping boisterously before a crucifix, 'in a fair church', she was arrested by the Mayor, who accused her of being 'a false strumpet, a false Lollard, and a false deceiver of the people'. The Steward of Leicester evidently held some such opinion of her, for when he privately questioned her, and wished to act lewdly towards her, he was so astonished at her unfeigned horror that, like many a man before, he said, 'Either thou art a right good woman, or else a right wicked one'. She was examined in the Articles of Faith by the Abbot of Leicester in the Church of All Hallows; her straightforward answers satisfied the ecclesiastical judges, but the Mayor was obdurate. He was convinced she was a Lollard, going about the country spreading poisonous doctrines, which would destroy the foundations of decent life and ordered government. He would only consent to her release when she promised to fetch at once from the Bishop of Lincoln 'a letter of discharge' that would relieve him of responsibility. When Margery, having resumed her travels, appeared in York, her dress, weeping, and bold words soon set rumours flying. Those answerable for the safety and peace of the city felt compelled to arrest her. After a preliminary examination in the Chapter-house of the Minister she was commanded to appear before the Archbishop at Cawood. This proved to be another of those striking occasions when this simple, untrained woman was able, by her boldness and sincerity, to outwit and outshine much cleverer men: her pert and pointed replies remind us repeatedly of Joan of Arc:

'Then the Archbishop said to her, "I am evil informed of thee. I hear it said that thou art a right wicked woman".

'And she answered back, "I also hear it said that ye are a wicked man. And if ye be as wicked as men say, ye shall never come to Heaven, unless ye amend whilst ye be here".

'Then he said full boisterously, "Why, thou (wretch), what say men of me?"

'She answered, "Other men, sir, can tell you well enough".

'Then said a great clerk with a furred hood, "Peace! Speak of thyself and let him be".'[1]

In the end the Archbishop treated her considerately; he gave one of his trusted servants five shillings 'to lead her fast out of this country'.

She went on to Bridlington, Hull, and Hessle; when about to cross the Humber, she was detained as a dangerous Lollard by two yeomen of the Duke of Bedford, who had set a price of £100 upon her head. When, at the Chapter-house of Beverley, she once more came before the Archbishop 'and many great clerks, priests, canons, and secular men', we are not surprised at His Grace's exclamation, 'What, woman! art thou come again? I would fain be delivered of thee!'[2] Two serious charges were laid against her. First, that she was carrying heretical letters about the country for the Arch-Lollard, Sir John Oldcastle (Lord Cobham); this she briefly but forcibly characterized as 'lies'. Second, that she had counselled Lady Greystoke, cousin-german to the Duke of Bedford, to forsake her husband, which was 'enough to be burnt for'. Margery's version was that she only told some edifying tales about loving one's enemies. Again the Archbishop dealt mercifully with her: besides letting her go, he gave her a letter with seal 'to record that neither error nor heresy had been proved against her'. After a servant had led her to the Humber, he returned, taking back with him the official letter.

When she had been to London to get from the Archbishop of Canterbury a letter of good character—which would serve also as a certificate of safe conduct—she settled for several years at Lynn. This extended stay was probably due to her state of health. Slander, poverty,

[1] p. 188.   [2] p. 197.

persecution, and imprisonment had reduced her to a pitiable condition. Persistent pains racked her body, sex-hallucinations tortured her mind, and her soul was wrapped in darkness because she thought she had offended God. Her attacks of weeping became more frequent and violent. She would completely lose control of herself, crying out, 'I die! I die!' while her face became livid, and she was bathed in sweat. A priest—a popular preacher—who came to Lynn, let it be known that he would not have her in his congregation. This, along with her afflictions, once more raised the old controversy as to the source of Margery's lachrymal fount: was it of God or the Devil? At this point of the record, Margery tries to justify her abundance of tears by reference to the cryings of St. Mary of Oignies, Bonaventura, Richard Rolle, and Elizabeth of Hungary. Perhaps Margery had studied these illustrious examples too well. Soon after this she received an intimation from the Lord, 'I shall take away thy crying, so that thou shalt no more cry so loud, nor in the manner that thou hast done before, even though thou wouldst'. Some said that this was the final proof that she had been all along 'a false feigned hypocrite'!

But throughout these distressful experiences Margery was wonderfully sustained by Divine Grace; and she could on occasion, by a display of courage and devotion, compel the grudging admiration of her detractors. When the Guildhall at Lynn was destroyed by fire (1421), the flames threatened not only the beloved parish church of St. Margaret, but also the whole town. Then people begged her to cry and sob to avert disaster. The priest-in-charge, after asking her advice, bore the Precious Sacrament as near to the fire as he could; but apparently it produced no effect, for Margery saw the sparks coming into the choir through the lantern of the church. She then besought God to quench the flames: the answer came—a snowstorm. She also became something of an oracle, being consulted on a variety of questions: concerning life, death, and eternity: about sickness, going on a journey, and the threat of pestilence. She was in great demand to pray over the dying; and her words of comfort to the bereaved were reported to be sweetly efficacious. There can be no doubt that she was regarded by many as a public benefactress.

One of the most affecting chapters in the book is that in which Margery describes the slow and pitiable ending of her husband's life. Whatever we may think about their agreement to separate, and the subsequent independent line taken by Margery, we shall admit that her steadfast devotion to her husband in his declining years was a splendid act of self-sacrifice, which, for any seeming previous neglect, made handsome amends. When John was 'a man in great age, passing three score years', he fell down stairs and seriously damaged himself, 'insomuch that he had in his head five linen plugs for many days'. When the wound had been stitched up, and it was possible to move him, Margery 'took home her husband with her and kept him years after, as long as he lived, and had full much labour with him; for in his last days he turned childish again, and lacked reason. . . .' He lost control of his limbs and organs; he could do nothing for himself, not even the simplest and most necessary acts. He required the same care and attention as an infant. At times Margery felt sick with loathing at some of her duties; yet, 'she served him, and helped him, as she thought, as she would have done Christ Himself'.[1]

This part of her life is aptly summed up in her words:

'So, by process of time, her mind and her thought was so joined to God that she never forgot Him, but continually had mind of Him and beheld Him in all creatures.'[2]

The second part of the book tells of her last great adven-

[1] pp. 264–6.   [2] p. 253.

ture, undertaken when she was over sixty: a journey to Germany. This enterprise also puts Margery before us in a favourable light, as, in spite of her fears of the perils and hardships of the unknown way, she was willing to go for the sake of charity. One of Margery's sons had been sent abroad as a foreign agent for a Lynn merchant. He had married a girl of Pruce,[1] in Dewcheland, and brought her on a visit to this country. Unfortunately, the day after his arrival, he was seized with sickness, and within a month, passed away. His widow remained here a year and a half; she then desired to return to her own people. Margery was inwardly instructed to go with her, but as she did not like the sea, she resisted the divine leading. In the end, without informing any one, she decided to obey. She and her daughter-in-law embarked at Ipswich. After a week's sailing, with two nights of terrible tempests, they were driven on to the coast of Norway; from there, after taking part in joyous Easter celebrations, they came, in calmer weather, to Danske.[2] In this ancient port, Margery soon made some friends, and stayed five or six weeks; her daughter-in-law went on home.

Before returning to England this active and hardy old lady determined to go once again on pilgrimage. She found a man who promised to act as guide. The first part of the journey, by sea to Strawissownd,[3] was safely accomplished; the second part, by land to Wilsnack,[4] presented many perils. The roads were infested with thieves. Margery's companion was mortally afraid. Because she

[1] Prussia. Dewcheland covered parts of present Germany, Holland, and Belgium.
[2] Danzig.
[3] Stralsund. Margery quaintly remarks: 'If the names of the places be not right written, let no man marvel, for she studied more about contemplation than the names of places, and him that wrote them had never seen them and therefore hold him excused.'
[4] In the Mark of Brandenburg. It illustrates a popular form of devotion of the later Middle Ages. In 1383 the church was destroyed by fire, but from the ruins three sacred hosts were rescued, and found to be blood-red in colour. A miracle was announced. Streams of pilgrims came from far and near.

could not go at his speed, he tried to desert her; but she besought him not to forsake her in those strange lands, especially 'as there was open war betwixt the English and those countries'. The man pushed on more rapidly than ever. In the effort to keep up with him, Margery must have broken down, had they not luckily come to a small hostelry, where they were detained for a couple of nights by violent weather; and although Margery could be provided with only a little straw for a bed, she felt it was a godsend. She completed the journey in a wain.

After a brief stay at Wilsnack, Margery and her guide, with other pilgrims, turned homewards. They rode towards Akun[1] in wagons. Once again, on account of her tears, Margery was deserted by her fellow-travellers, including her guide; and alone, in a strange town, she had to endure the raillery of certain priests:

'They called her "English sterte", and spoke many lewd words unto her, shewing uncleanly expression and behaviour, proffering to lead her about if she would.'[2]

She was compelled to finish the journey to Akun in rather unsavoury company; but her brief and frank description of her companions gives us another unadorned picture of the medieval roads:

'When they were outside the towns, her fellowship took off their clothes, and sitting naked, picked themselves. Need compelled her to await them and prolong her journey and be at much more cost than she would otherwise have been. This creature was ashamed to put off her clothes as her fellows did, and therefore, through her communing, had part of their vermin and was bitten and stung full evil, both day and night, till God sent her other fellowship. She kept on with her fellowship with great anguish and discomfort and much delay, until they came to Akun."[3]

[1] Aachen.
[2] p. 324: 'sterte' means 'tail': a Dutch term of abuse for the English, who they believed had tails.
[3] p. 325.

Margery 'abode there ten or else eleven days to see Our Lady's smock and other holy relics shown on St. Margaret's Day'. Having been unexpectedly left behind by 'a worshipful woman of London', she was obliged to ask two London men if she might travel with them; but these hastened so fast that when they came to the next town she attached herself to another group of pilgrims. She was no better off; for these, having been robbed and possessing but little money, were in a great hurry to get home. At last this marvellous old lady had to make a confession which must have wrung her heart:

'Afterwards they all went on together. The said creature came soon behind: she was too aged and too weak to hold foot with them. She ran and leapt as fast as she might till her might failed. Then she spake with the poor friar whom she had cheered before, offering to requite his costs till he came to Caleys,[1] if he would abide with her and let her go with him till they came there, and yet give him reward for his labour. He was well content and consented to her desire.'[2]

But Margery was now thoroughly fatigued. She passed weary days and wretched nights. Late one evening, 'they happed to come under a woodside, busily looking if they might espy any place wherein they might rest'. The friar occupied a barn; Margery, still fearful for her chastity, passed a miserable night lying on a heap of bracken. The final stage of the journey to Caleys found Margery completely spent. For two dreary days they trudged through deep sand, over hills and down valleys, suffering acutely from hunger and thirst; Margery 'thought her spirit would have departed from her body as she went on the way'. In Caleys she found friends who provided her with a home, with food and drink, and a change of garments. Her gratitude was unbounded. The friar, with the promised reward and Margery's warmest thanks, went on his way.

[1] Calais.   [2] p. 328.

After an uneventful passage to Dover, Margery made her way through Canterbury to London, now 'clad in a cloth of canvas, as it were a sacken apron, as she had gone beyond the sea'. Many turned to look,

'inasmuch as she was not clad as she would like to have been, for lack of money. She, desiring to go unknown till such time as she might arrange to borrow some money, bore a kerchief before her face. Notwithstanding that she did so, some dissolute persons, supposing it was Mar. Kempe of Lynne[1], said, so that she might easily hear, these words of reproof; "Ah! thou false flesh, thou shalt no good meat eat".'[2]

This saying, attributed to Margery, and twisted into various forms, had become 'a manner of proverb'; but she declares it was invented by the Devil, the father of lies. As so often, she found good folk who offered her both friendship and hospitality. In the warmth of this kindness her spirit soon revived, and the fires of enthusiasm began again to burn:

'She spoke boldly and mightily wheresoever she went in London, against swearers, banners, liars, and such other vicious people, against the pompous array, both of men and women.'[3]

From London she went to Sheen, three days before Lammas Day, 'to purchase her pardon through the mercy of Our Lord'; from thence, in the company of Reynald, a young hermit, she went on home:

'When she was come home to Lynne, she made obedience to her confessor. He gave her full sharp words, for she was his obedience, and had taken upon herself such a journey without his knowledge. Therefore he was moved the more against her, but Our Lord helped her so that she had as good love of him, and of other friends after, as she had before, worshipped be God. Amen.'[4]

In conclusion, a brief word must be said about the

[1] The only place in which her surname occurs in the book.
[2] P. 335.
[3] P. 337.
[4] p. 341.

media of Margery's supernatural communications: her visions, locutions, and intuitions. Their tone and substance, being entirely free from mawkish elements, are beyond reproach. Some passages are of an elevated moral nature, and give valuable hints for holy living; others are of a rare devotional charm, and will help to put our soul into the right attitude for high endeavours. The qualities of these spiritual exchanges which most strike one are their fervour, intimacy, and reality. As with other warm-hearted mystics, so with Margery, 'the fire of love' was a favourite phrase to express the rapture of the soul in fellowship with the Beloved. Margery's consciousness of this is so overflowing that she communicates something of its fulness to the reader. The same is true of the unforced familiarity of these interchanges: all barriers were down, seeker and Sought were one. Some of these conversations, too, have such an air of actuality that you can easily imagine yourself a participator. The terms of address throughout are most frequently domestic—marital, filial, and parental.

We do not claim for Margery's heavenly communications any great illuminative value. In this respect they differ from Julian's: they are on nothing like the same intellectual level. In her spiritual commerce Julian did actually receive light on important theological problems, like the existence of evil, the meaning of pain, and the use of prayer. The fruits of Julian's divinely-guided meditations on some of the mysteries of the Faith will always be cherished by souls in search of Truth. Margery claimed to receive light, but it was more personal; it related mainly to problems of her own conduct, and to matters like foretelling the future, and the predestination of souls. From the speculative point of view, Margery does not contribute a single fresh idea.

The scheme of her visions is not hard to detect. All devout believers were taught in their meditations to use concrete images; to select some incident in the life of Christ—particularly His Passion—and to think about it in such a realistic way as to make them feel they were present. That would be Margery's method. To help her imagination she would seize on objects about her. Hence her visions, in structure, contents, and colour, resembled the many works of art upon which she daily gazed: illuminations of missals, stained glass in church windows, statuary, and the Stations of the Cross. She owed not a little to the picturesque scenery of the Miracle Plays; the very language of the Plays can also be heard in the conversations between herself and her heavenly visitants. We cannot but admire the skilful use that Margery made of these sources. I confess that in reading these simple but vivid accounts of her meditations and contemplations, my heart is strangely moved.

For one fact we are deeply indebted to Margery—her insistence that Love is the key to all the mysteries of life. She was a good woman, and tried to lead a useful life; but her course was not smooth. She suffered much, and saw much suffering about her: many acts of wanton cruelty are described in her book. Yet she never doubted that behind the blood, and wounds, and tears of the world, there was ever beating the Heart of Eternal Love. Perhaps the chief value of her book is the reiteration of this fact. And that is why we can concur in these words of her Lord, 'Daughter, by this book, many a man shall be turned to Me and believe there-in'.[1]

[1] p. 368.